GIRL

Love, Sex, Romance,

and Being You

Magination Press • Washington, DC
American Psychological Association

by **Karen Rayne, PhD**

*This book is dedicated to my family, who are special in the most empowering,
creative, and challenging ways possible: Julia, Arwyn, Vivian, Robert, and my
beautiful wife, Nyk —KR*

Published by

MAGINATION PRESS®
An Educational Publishing Foundation Book
American Psychological Association
750 First Street NE
Washington, DC 20002

Magination Press is a registered trademark of the
American Psychological Association.

For more information about our books, including a complete
catalog, please write to us, call 1-800-374-2721, or visit our
website at www.apa.org/pubs/magination.

Book design by Gwen Grafft
Illustrations by Ramsey Beyer
Anatomical illustrations by Nyk Rayne

Printed by Sheridan, Chelsea, MI

Library of Congress Cataloging-in-Publication Data
Names: Rayne, Karen, author.
Title: Girl : love, sex, romance, and being you / by Karen Rayne, PhD.
Other titles: Love, sex, romance, and being you
Description: Washington, DC : Magination Press, [2017] | Includes
    bibliographical references and index. | Audience: Age 15+. |
    "American Psychological Association."
Identifiers: LCCN 2016050563 (print) | LCCN 2017007026 (ebook) |
    ISBN 9781433823398 (pbk.) | ISBN 143382339X (pbk.) |
    ISBN 9781433827730 () | ISBN 1433827735
Subjects: LCSH: Teenage girls—Conduct of life—Juvenile literature. |
    Sex instruction for girls—Juvenile literature. | Sex instruction for
    teenagers—Juvenile literature.
Classification: LCC HQ798 .R39 2017 (print) | LCC HQ798 (ebook) |
    DDC 155.5/33—dc23
LC record available at https://lccn.loc.gov/2016050563

Manufactured in the United States of America
10 9 8 7 6 5 4 3 2 1

Advance Praise

This should be a go-to book for all girls. In addition to providing straightforward, smart advice on all the right topics, the book promotes self-awareness, self-confidence, and self-acceptance, all of which are so important for preparing girls to have healthy romantic and sexual relationships. The inclusion of insight-building questions for girls to really get to know themselves, as well as other young people writing about their own experiences, makes this book "alive" and very real. If there is a young girl in your life that you care about, go out and buy her this book.

—Joanne Davila, PhD
Professor of Psychology, Stony Brook University
Author of *The Thinking Girl's Guide to the Right Guy: How Knowing Yourself Can Help You Navigate Dating, Hookups, and Love*

This book is full of useful, relevant, accurate information for girl-identi-fied people. It is sexuality education at its best, presented in a way that treats young people as competent decision-makers and moral agents. Especially important, the book maintains a realistic and sex-positive tone throughout. Highly recommended.

—Rev. Marie Alford-Harkey
President and CEO, Religious Institute

Karen Rayne understands the world today's teens live in. And she's a fabulous sexuality educator. In *GIRL: Love, Sex, Romance, and Being You*, she breaks it all down in a way that will help older teen girls understand the straightforward and complicated pieces of love, sex, and dating, and then helps girls put those pieces together in ways that help girls respect and be true to themselves.

—Andrew P. Smiler, PhD
Author of *Challenging Casanova: Beyond the Stereotype of the Promiscuous Young Male* and *Dating and Sex: A Guide for the 21st Century Teen Boy*

I LOVE this book! Truly, I have been waiting for a book like this. *GIRL* is comprehensive and the topics are covered so thoroughly—it is quite im-pressive just how much Dr. Rayne includes in each chapter. *GIRL* will be a major contribution to psychological literature and self-help YA, and will be something that teen girls will treasure!

—Bonnie Zucker, PsyD
Author of *Anxiety-Free Kids* and *Take Control of OCD*;
Co-author of *Resilience Builder Program for Children and Adolescents*

GIRL is thoughtful, thorough, and a treat to read. Karen compassionately balances accurate, helpful information with the inclusion of different experiences and identities to create a book capable of making everyone's life happier, healthier, and better understood.

—Sam Killermann
Author of *A Guide to Gender: The Social Justice Advocate's Handbook, 2nd Edition* and of the "It's Pronounced Metrosexual" blog: www.itspronouncedmetrosexual.com

GIRL is like overhearing conversations between a teen and her really cool older sisters. Topics include relationship and sexuality basics as well as issues rarely addressed, such as cross-cultural perspectives on sex and the importance of honoring your own personality, body, and interests. The book brims with authentic and empowering messages, including my favorite: "Sex is beautiful, pleasure is beautiful, and orgasm is beautiful."

—Melanie Davis, PhD, CSE, CSES

GIRL brings a unique and authentic voice to the global conversation about human sexuality. As young women are coming into their own, navigating their identities and sexual and romantic connections, they need all kinds of support. Dr. Rayne brings empathy, information, kindness, and guidance for teens while encouraging them to listen to and develop their own voice. It's a must-read!

—Sara Nasserzadeh, PhD
Author of *Sexuality Education Wheel of Context: A Guide for Sexuality Educators, Advocates and Researchers*

About the Author

Karen Rayne, PhD, is an educator, trainer, and nationally recognized expert on sexuality. Karen lives in Austin, TX, where she works with people of all ages to make information and conversations about sexuality accessible. Her goal is to ensure everyone has someone to talk with about sexuality and a place to find honest, accurate information. Because she can't talk with everyone, she writes books like this one.

About Magination Press

Magination Press is an imprint of the American Psychological Association, the largest scientific and professional organization representing psychologists in the United States and the largest association of psychologists worldwide.

Contents

Dear Reader 8

Introduction 9

Biology and Being a Girl

Chapter 1   Who Are You? 15

Chapter 2   Gender and Identity 29

Chapter 3   Attraction 47

Chapter 4   Inside and Outside Bodies 65

Chapter 5   STIs and Prevention 89

Chapter 6   Pregnancy and Prevention 107

Dating and Relationships

Chapter 7   Decision Making 129

Chapter 8   Communication 143

Chapter 9   Healthy Relationships 101 157

Chapter 10   Hooking Up 171

Chapter 11   Dating or Starting a "Thing" 183

Chapter 12   Being in a Relationship 193

Chapter 13   Ending Relationships 205

Chapter 14   Consent, Harassment,
                    Sexual Assault, and Rape 219

Sex and Sex

Chapter 15   Your First Time 243

Chapter 16   Orgasms 257

Chapter 17   Masturbation 275

Chapter 18   Foreplay, Making Out, and Attraction 291

Chapter 19   Oral, Anal, and Vaginal Sex 301

Chapter 20   Fantasy, Kink, and Pornography 311

What Now?

Chapter 21   Books vs. Real Life 329
Chapter 22   Sexuality Is a Lifelong Thing 335

Anatomy Glossary 347
Bibliography 353
Index 356

GIRL

Love, Sex, Romance,

and Being You

Dear Reader,

It is my deepest hope that you are here because you want to think about what being a girl means physically, emotionally, and sexually.

But first, it is important that we consider some of the cultural assumptions that are made about girls. Girls can be told, at different times, to be sensitive, strong, emotional, bold, sexually pure while still sexually attractive, and so much more. Let's throw those cultural assumptions out the window. This book is about the incredible range of what being a girl means.

This book is for all young women—of all bodies and sexualities—and is written with love and respect for each individual's process.

I'm glad you're here.

Karen Rayne, PhD

Introduction

Welcome to *GIRL*!

The content in this book is honest, real-world information for older teenagers who identify as female. Do you have questions about sex, love, relationships, and jumping from high school to college, all while navigating your sexuality? That's what we're here to talk about!

I hope that reading this book is so much fun for you. Sex, love, and romance can bring beauty to life, if they're done in ways that are right for the people involved. Below is some information that will come in handy as you read this book.

Words

The language around sex and sexuality is so important. There are a lot of words, from anatomy to psychology to culturally evolving words. If you don't know the definition of a word, don't let this intimidate you. Many of the chapters start with defining words that are important to that particular topic; if you come across a word that you don't know that isn't defined in the book, just do a quick Internet search for it.

The language around sexuality, particularly as it applies to identity, is changing quickly. If there are words about identity that feel outdated, replace them with words that resonate for you.

Parents

When I talk about parents, I'm referring to the people who raised you, whoever that means to you. Sometimes parents are biological and sometimes they're not. The parent-teen relationship is much more important than any kind of biological connection. So if you have a different word or name that you use for your parents, I hope you'll think about them whenever I say *parents*. You can even take a pen and write in the person who is meaningful to you.

Additional Resources

At the end of each chapter are additional resources. These point to books, websites, blog posts, TED talks, and more. Because the range of topics in this book is so large, some of the topics had so many additional resources that it was hard to narrow it down to just a few, while for other topics it was hard to find even one or two resources to recommend. But know that what I did include in these sections are some of the best available at the writing of this book.

Here is a key to the Additional Resources icons:

📖 Represents books   📱 Represents apps

📖 Represents websites   🖥 Represents organizations

📞 Represents hotlines

Parts of the Book

There are a lot of little interactive and complementary "extras" scattered throughout the chapters. Here's a run-down of some of them.

The Q's

Throughout the book, there are questions for you to think about and, ideally, answer. These questions will hopefully help you check your knowledge, think about your feelings, and question what it is that you really want and need. There are different ways you can think about these questions:

• Consider possible answers to the questions, without writing them down.

• Write the answers in the book or in a journal or diary.

• Talk about your answers with a friend, counselor, or other trusted person.

The Diary Entries

Each chapter includes diary entries written by teenage girls and young adults. These diary entries are to show you how different girls relate to and live with the different topics covered in each chapter every day. These are real people writing about their real experiences. Some of them are writing under their own names, some under a pen name. To give you a sense of their personalities, the drawings of the authors are how they really look.

Here are introductions to each of the authors:

- **Anjali** is a full-time reproductive health professional, a part-time photographer, and an Indian classical dancer. She can't live without coffee, chocolate, and food. Anjali bounces between DC and Baltimore and loves all things in the reproductive health and sexual health realms. She hopes to one day travel and eat her way across the world!

- **Blake** is a queer/non-binary femme activist, artist, survivor, and performer who has a penchant for being silly. They work as a teaching artist and enjoy musical improv, acro yoga, and being a sponge. A native Texan, Blake grew up in Dallas and attended the University of Texas earning a bachelor of arts in theatre and dance, and a certificate in LGBTQ studies. It is their dream to create a holistic trauma healing center in New York for people experiencing homelessness.

- **Erin** is a theologian currently living in California where she is studying for a master's degree in Women's Studies in Religion at Claremont Graduate University. She also happens to be lesbian and transgender. A 2016 graduate of Eastern University in Pennsylvania, Erin earned her bachelor's degree in Biblical studies. She enjoys reading, spending time with her friends and family, and being in the snow. Erin hopes to return to the East Coast after completing her master's program.

- **Jordan** loves long walks on the beach, Harry Potter, and smashing the patriarchy. She is also a proud lover of theatre who would totally go to acting school if she didn't hate uncertainty so much. Instead, she's majoring in social work in college, and she eventually plans to be a clinical sexologist. Jordan dislikes queerphobia, institutionalized racism, fat prejudice, the fact that she'll probably still be paying off student loans on her 80th birthday, and things that are grape-flavored.

If Jordan could choose three people to be her besties, they would be Tess Holliday, Nicki Minaj, and Emma Watson. Finally, she hopes that other girls can identify with her diary entries, and that they give comfort to people who are going through the same things she has.

- **Lina G.** is a 22-year-old single mother working on multiple screenplays and a blog. During high school, her closest friends consisted of the popular and promiscuous girls, although she herself was neither of those things. As an undercover bisexual at a Christian-based boarding school, she struggled with self-acceptance, but she has recently learned to love and appreciate her true self.

- **Margaret** is 20 years old and attending her first semester at Borough of Manhattan Community College. Her major is early childhood education, to further her future career of secondary special education. When she isn't going to school, she works as a peer educator for Grand Street Settlement and at your neighborhood 7-Eleven. She really has a passion for working with children with special needs, and has had experience in that particular field since she was 13 years old. Dyeing her hair different colors as often as the seasons change, she is at times quirky, extremely weird, and fun to be around.

These diary entries are one of my favorite parts of the book. I hope you enjoy them, too!

Endmatter
At the end of the book is a section with additional information, including an anatomy glossary, and an index of the content in the entire book. These are great resources to refer to as you're reading the book or any time you hear something you'd like more information about.

And now? Dive in! Have fun.

Chapter 1

Who Are You?

This chapter is all about what it means to be a girl, inside and out, biologically, psychologically, and sexually. It is about the way you describe yourself through your words, activities, appearance, friends, social media, work, school . . . everything! Taken together, these things impact the way you feel and the way other people react to you. Figuring out who you are is important, and so is deciding how to represent yourself to all the other people in your life and online.

Brand

Branding is about communication through words and pictures and how they fit together. We often think about branding as it applies to advertised products—but branding also applies to you and how you represent yourself to others. There are at least two places where you probably present yourself to people: online and in person. But in both of those general locations, there are many actual places, including social media networks, text messages, email, family groups, friend groups, work, and school, to name a few. You will likely represent yourself somewhat differently in these different circles. For example, you probably choose to use different words with your grandparents than you do with your closest friends.

For the purpose of this book, we're calling in-person interactions "face-to-face," or f2f for short. The questions and issues associated with online and f2f interactions have many similarities, but they also have some differences, so we'll talk about them separately.

Your f2f Life

Your f2f life is tied up in so many people, relationships, responsibilities, and desires that influence your home, school, work, and more. You

probably highlight or downplay certain aspects of yourself in each particular setting, which means you're balancing a lot of different ways of
being you over any given week or even over a single day. Or, although
rare, you might be exactly the same in all situations.

f2f Situation Q's

1. How many different places in your life call for different versions of you? Take a second to write out a list.

2. Consider who you are in each of those settings. Is
   that who you want to be in that setting?

How you portray yourself in each area of your life is based on your
identities, physical appearance, what you say and how you choose
to say it, and your nonverbal communication. Everything you talk
about matters in this regard, including your interests, religious beliefs,
friends, romantic partners, and family. Taken together, these things
and how you present them influence other people's perceptions of
you, both positively and negatively.

Your Identities

Identities are sometimes visible and sometimes invisible, but regardless, they influence how you interact with the world. Do you feel like
your identities help you feel included? Do you feel like your identities
are different from the people around you in ways that makes you feel
separate? Do the feelings of inclusivity or separateness feel good or
bad to you? The answers to these questions, both for you and for the
people around you, are starting points for the ways you will interact.

For example, when someone looks different from the people
around them, whether because of their race, religion, gender, clothing,
or something else, they may be a target for teasing, bullying, and worse.
Alternatively, the people around them could consider what it means to
be that person, from a place of understanding and love. Invisible

identities are sometimes even more complicated than visible ones because whether or not to disclose them becomes an issue. More on that later.

There is potential for both beautiful things and painful things to come from our identities. When everyone is able to approach themselves and others with love—not in spite of their identities but because of them—the world will be a better place.

Your Language

Language is the easiest way to see how we present ourselves differently based on the situation; there are different *appropriate* and *inappropriate* words or phrases or text speak to use with friends, parents, teachers, and bosses. There are norms that each situation calls for. If you worry that it's bad to present yourself differently in varying situations, think about how different presentations in word choice are considered appropriate and are often expected. You will speak differently at a party or on the job, and the people in those situations will expect different kinds of information and interactions from you. The same is also true of all of the other ways you present yourself that we talk about in this chapter.

Your Nonverbals

The ways you communicate through body language and facial expression are just as important as the words you use. Think of body language and facial expressions like the emojis of f2f communication—the only difference is they're not optional; your face and body language mirror the emotion you're feeling. Whether or not you make eye contact, how smooth or irregular your breathing is, whether your shoulders are pulled down or pushed back all say something about how you feel in that moment. Two important things about nonverbal communication:

1. It's very cultural. For example: A student making eye contact with their teacher in the United States is considered respectful; but if a student makes eye contact with their teacher in China, it is considered disrespectful.

2. Some people have a knack for understanding nonverbal communication; other people don't. If it comes easily to you, that's great! If it doesn't, you'll have to learn the trends, but that's not an impossible task. There are many online resources that outline the details of nonverbal communication in dominant Westernized cultures[1].

It can be difficult to find explicit discussions of nonverbal communication norms in other communities and cultures, but they do exist. Quietly listening, watching, and asking for help from leaders and mentors within the communities and cultures where you live and work may provide an effective way of learning.

Your Physical Appearance

Why does it matter what you look like? Partly because of the connection between identities and physical appearance, and partly because the first thing that other people know about you is usually what you look like. They'll make assumptions about your dreadlocks and your pixie cut, your flip-flops and your Birkenstocks, your neckties and your earrings. Some of those assumptions might be true, while some of those assumptions will absolutely be false. No one shares everything about themselves through their physical appearance.

It's likely that you make at least small changes to your physical appearance based on the activity that you're doing or the people whom you're meeting—which is as it should be. Different activities call for different shoe choices, like hiking in a forest and walking on a beach. But other parts of your appearance—like your haircut, hair color, or facial piercings—don't change as easily as your shoes. Sometimes you may make choices based on what other people want of you, like not wearing your running shoes to a wedding, but for the most part, it is usually better to stay true to what feels good and right to you, rather than anyone else.

Your Interests

Your interests—whether they are objects, hobbies, career ambitions, art, or people—speak to who you are. Other people will make assumptions about you based on your interests—broad assumptions, like whether

---

[1]For example, see: https://www.verywell.com/nonverbal-communication-4012932

or not you will succeed in life, and specific assumptions, like whether or not you should be friends. Having mutual interests can be useful for friendships, so these assumptions are useful, however any assumptions about your future successes and failures aren't relevant if they're based on your interests alone. For example, just because you play soccer or the flute doesn't mean you'll want to do these things professionally. The way that people define success, whether by happiness or money or something else, can really vary from person to person.

Sometimes people have interests that must be temporarily put on hold. For example, you might decide not to date or have sex until you move out of your parents' home because it would put your relationship with them, and potentially your wellbeing, at risk. Or, you might decide that you're too busy during finals week to go to your usual Monday night dance class. It can be a good thing to wait until the time is right to pursue your interests. Never lose sight of yourself, but always remember that you can go after your interests if they remain important to you later on.

Your People

The people whom you spend time with—your family, friends, bosses, and co-workers—influence you and people's understanding of who you are. While it's true that we can be friends with people who are very different from us, it's more common to be friends with people who have similarities in life. If more of your friends are employed than unemployed, you are more likely to think about getting a job. If your friends are mostly open-minded about gender and sexual identity, you are more likely to be open-minded than if your friends adhere to standard gender roles and norms. You're also more likely to decide to have sex if most of your friends are having sex. Most people understand this, and so they make assumptions that people are usually more similar to, rather than less similar to, their friends and family.

THIS YEAR FOR SHAKESPEARIENCE, WE'RE GOING TO SPIN MACBETH, HAMLET, WINTER'S TALE, & TWELFTH NIGHT INTO SKITS THAT SHOW HOW WE ACT DIFFERENTLY WHEN WE'RE ALONE VS. BEING WATCHED & RECORDED. I HAVE THE BEST PART, HONESTLY; I'M THE PORTER FROM MACBETH, SO ALL I HAVE TO DO IS ACT DRUNK & MAKE SEX JOKES. ANYWAY, OUR DIRECTOR ASKED US QUESTIONS ABOUT OUR SOCIAL MEDIA INTERACTIONS TO GET US INTO THE 21ST CENTURY SPIRIT, & MANY TOPICS WERE BROUGHT UP: GENERAL DRAMA & SUBTWEETING, THE USE OF TEXTING & KIK TO BREAK UP WITH SIGNIFICANT OTHERS, INSTAGRAM ACCOUNTS CREATED TO EMBARRASS/MAKE FUN OF PEOPLE, ETC. THE BASIC THEME OF IT WAS THAT SOCIAL MEDIA IS BOTH AWESOME & THE BANE OF EVERYONE'S EXISTENCE. I LIKED THE CONVERSATION, BUT I WAS SILENT THE WHOLE TIME.

FOR CONTEXT, MY GENERAL REACTION TO THE BS DRAMA THAT MY FRIENDS SEEM TO ALWAYS BE MIXED IN WITH IS "LOL." I'VE NEVER BEEN INVOLVED WITH THAT CRAP. THE BIGGEST "DRAMA" I'VE EVER BEEN IN WAS WHEN SOME ACQUAINTENCE CALLED ME FAT & UGLY IN SOPHOMORE YEAR. FOR ME, WATCHING MY PEERS FLAIL ABOUT ANGRILY BECAUSE OF DRAMA IS LIKE WATCHING MONKEYS SCREAM AT EACH OTHER AT THE ZOO— GENERALLY ENTERTAINING WITH A SIDE OF DISAPPOINTMENT. I ALWAYS GO THROUGH THE STRINGS OF TWEETS & PASSIVE-AGGRESSIVE FACEBOOK POSTS, BUT NO ONE EVER DRAGS ME DOWN INTO IT. THAT'S PROBABLY BECAUSE I'VE NEVER BEEN "POPULAR," & MY FOLLOWING ON SOCIAL MEDIA HAS ALWAYS BEEN QUITE MEAGER. I DON'T CARE TOO MUCH ABOUT IT, & I'M GLAD THAT I DON'T CARE. I DON'T JUDGE OTHERS FOR WANTING MORE SOCIAL MEDIA ATTENTION; I KNOW WHAT IT'S LIKE TO WANT TO BE NOTICED & APPRECIATED FOR MY WORDS. BUT SOCIAL MEDIA JUST ISN'T MY THING. ANYWAY, I LIKE HOW THE CONVERSATION IS GOING TO SET THE STAGE FOR THE REHEARSAL PROCESS. & I'M SUPER HYPE TO BE IN A SHAKESPEARE PERFORMANCE THAT INCLUDES SMARTPHONES.

JORDAN

This isn't to say that there aren't people who go against the trends of their friends, families, or peer groups, because there are. But if you are different from the people around you, you'll have to make it clear when you want someone to see you differently.

f2f Q's

1. Are you unhappy with, or do you feel not really yourself, in the places or with the groups you spend time?

2. Are there ways that you can be more yourself?

Your Online Life

Online is a unique kind of place that isn't really a *place*. Most people in the United States have some kind of social media account where they create online content about themselves with pictures and descriptions of their thoughts, feelings, and activities. At the time that I am writing this book, Instagram, Snapchat, Twitter, and a few others are the most common social media platforms. Most online interactions, including texting and social media, serve the same purpose as connecting with friends f2f. Given how quickly the online world changes, it might be that all or some of these specific platforms have lost their appeal by the time you read this, even if you're only reading it a year or two after I wrote it. What I say going forward has nothing at all to do with which online platform you're using or how you're texting. Instead, this section is about expressing yourself digitally, the things you need to think about, and why and how it's different from expressing yourself in f2f situations.

Being You Online

Representing yourself online seems to and can be pretty straightforward. You post words or photos of the things around you or repost things that other people have posted. Ideally, those words and pictures are meaningful, funny, informative, thoughtful, or connecting. Most teenagers (and most people, regardless of their age) use online communication to stay in touch with people who  aren't physically around them. Teenagers especially need this kind of connection because they usually aren't able to control where they are or who they're with as much as adults. So yay for social media letting you talk to your friends!

But it's not always that simple. You might have a really hard or sad day, but you don't want your friends or your parents to know. So you post something funny or happy as a way of covering up your bad feelings. Or maybe it's more about what other people are saying or doing online, making you feel sad, lonely, or confused. Maybe a particular person always seems to have the most perfect pictures and you feel like your life isn't so great compared to theirs. Or maybe they're trash talking a friend of yours and you don't know how to respond.

Being online doesn't make feelings of sadness, envy, or fear of missing out bigger or smaller—these feelings are probably present in your f2f life as well. The main difference is it's usually more difficult to get away from these feelings when you are online. Social media reminds us of our feelings, good or bad, constantly. However, you are probably just as likely to smile f2f when you don't feel very smiley as you are to put up a cheery post when it's not how you actually feel. You are certainly just as likely to feel hurt or unsure of how to respond if someone said something harsh or negative to you f2f as you are online. Still, negative online interactions can be harsher and more problematic because they are often also public. Managing these emotions and figuring out how you want to react, both online and f2f, is something that takes time—it could be something you continue to revisit your entire life.

Problems People Face Online

A woman named danah boyd (she prefers the lowercase spelling) has done great research on social media and texting—especially when it comes to teens. She emphasizes the importance of thinking about the following four things when communicating online:

1. **Online communication is persistent.** Online content has the potential to stick around forever, even if you delete it. It's easy for someone else to screenshot or otherwise grab anything that is posted online—and this includes apps like Snapchat, where content is supposedly deleted immediately. Anything you have stored digitally, even if you don't post it online, can be easily downloaded or saved to someone else's computer or phone. For example, say your device breaks and you take it to get repaired; you are trusting that the repairperson will refrain from looking through your files and saving whichever ones they want. This differs from f2f because, as long as something isn't recorded, interactions can only be saved as memories.

2. **Online communication is shareable.** Once something is saved in digital form, it can be easily shared. Your social media posts can be reposted. Or, worse, they can be saved, stored, and shared any time in the future. Memories that come from f2f experiences are different because they are never completely accurate and may even be entirely made up. That may be better or worse, depending on the situation.

3. **Online communication is visible.** Once something has been captured in a digital format, it can be seen by anyone online. This includes your immediate circle of family and friends, but also future friends, college admissions staff, your children, every boss you will have for the rest of your life, and more. It is potentially visible forever, because it is so persistent. This is different from f2f life, where something is only visible by the people who are present at a given moment in time.

4. **Online communication is searchable.** Once something exists online, it is searchable through Google or other platforms. You are searchable by name, your online account name, and your photo. An image search of a picture of your face will pull up all of the other pictures of your face online. This means that even pictures that aren't connected to your name in any way might be connected with you in the future. F2f interactions that are not recorded and uploaded are, obviously not searchable.

If you have a firm understanding of these four differences between f2f and online communications, you can make decisions about what you say, post, and do online that will hopefully keep your content from having a negative effect on you now or in the future. However, other people may post things about you or tag you in ways that you don't like—that's much harder to control and would take a whole book to talk about. For example, if someone has sexually suggestive pictures of you, those images are no longer under your control. You may have sent the pictures in good faith, and at a good time in your relationship, but if your relationship sours, that person may not respect your wishes. Do an Internet search for "revenge porn" to get an idea of how posting non-consensual pictures can cause a lot of trouble.

As the people who grew up online grow into adults, the way that everyone thinks about being online is going to change. Younger people have more experience being online at a younger age than older adults, therefore they are more likely to be understanding of pictures of teenagers doing stupid things. They will be less likely to assume that just because an adult has old pictures of themselves online, for example, drinking and driving, that they are still likely to drink and drive and so shouldn't be trusted. We can't know exactly what that will look like, but future adults are likely to be a little kinder and less judgmental about someone's digital footprint than adults are now. Other potential changes are new laws that could let people control the online information connected to them. The European Union has instituted new privacy laws as of mid-2016, but the United States hasn't begun to look into bringing the same protections to this country. So you shouldn't rely on this change quite yet—it might be a long time before the United States has such regulations on the books.

You can read more about danah boyd's ideas about being online and digital communication in her book *It's Complicated: The Social Lives of Networked Teens*. You can buy a copy pretty much anywhere, but you can also download it for free: http://www.danah.org/books /ItsComplicated.pdf.

Online Q's

1. Are you generally the same in how you present yourself online and f2f?

2. How are you different in different online platforms? How are you different in different f2f places?

3. What's the most uncomfortable you've ever been in an online interaction? How might you have made it more comfortable? Could you have walked away from the interaction? How might you have gotten help from someone else in making it more comfortable?

4. Knowing that online content is persistent, shareable, searchable, and visible, do you feel uncomfortable about anything that you've ever put online, texted, or had on your computer or phone?

5. How can you make sure that your online communications going forward are okay being persistent, shareable, searchable, and visible?

Online or f2f, It's All About Knowing and Doing You

Or at least it should be. You should be able to be happy, sad, sexy, disgruntled, and everything in between, as well as follow your interests in everything from surfing to earning money to running for elected office to basket weaving—all when and how you want to.

Ideally, in a perfect world, you would dress and speak and act in the ways that feel most authentically you all of the time and you would be loved and welcomed for it. Most people find reality a little less supportive; some people find reality far, far less supportive. What you decide to do with that support or lack thereof depends on a bunch of things. It's common to be accepted for some parts of who you are, but not for other parts, which varies depending on whom you're with. For example, your parents might be overwhelmingly supportive of you being a theater geek, but try to stop you from expressing yourself with short skirts. Some classmates might roll their eyes at you being in theater, but think your skirts are pretty cute.

So what do you do with people's reactions to who you are? It depends on what is important to you. Maybe you don't care that much about the short skirts—they just didn't look half bad at the store so you got them. Because you don't care about wearing them, you shrug when your parents say they don't like the skirts and you wear something else. But maybe you feel the skirts are an integral part of who you are. In that case, maybe they're worth arguing with your parents about. Or maybe you compromise and wear tights or leggings under the skirts. But those are, generally speaking, your three options: go with the other person's flow, stand firm, or try and compromise. It's likely that you'll do each of these at different points in time, based on a complex assessment of what is important to you, to the other person, and a bunch of other factors.

Short skirts are, usually, a minor thing to change. The bigger heartbreaks come with things that are essential to who you are as a person, like your sexual or gender identity, or your need to write and create art, or spending time with the person you've fallen in love with.

Figuring out how to go with another person's flow, compromising, or standing firm when it is about something that is so, so important to you—but your relationship with the other person is also so, so important to you—is really, really hard. Sometimes you might decide that your relationship with your parents, who provide you with shelter, food, and many other necessities, must take priority until you're old enough to support yourself, at which point you can be yourself. Sometimes that isn't an option, and being yourself has to come before anyone and anything else. Only you know which is more important and more practical in the moment. If you decide that someone else takes priority at a certain time, don't forget who you are. Keep that important part of yourself safe so it will still be there when you are finally independent and supporting yourself.

Additional Resources

Here are some resources on identity, discovering who you are, and being authentic:

- 📖 *Poetry Speaks Who I Am: Poems of Discovery, Inspiration, Independence, and Everything Else (A Poetry Speaks Experience)* by Elise Paschen and Dominique Raccah

- 💻 "Who Am I? A Philosophical Inquiry," a TED talk by Amy Adkins (http://ed.ted.com/lessons/who-am-i-a-philosophical-inquiry-amy-adkins)

- 💻 Rookie (http://www.rookiemag.com/)

I feel like my appearance couldn't be further from what I want. I am going to homecoming this weekend and I went to my cousin's house to get my "practice" make-up done (like it's my fucking wedding or something) and I look like every other cheerleader, bible-humping mom. I am white, thin, a cheerleader, and have long, blond hair, so everyone expects me to be this typical "cheerleader" type. No one knows that I have a girlfriend, on weekends go into the city and spend hours hooking up with B., or plan on looking drastically different than I do now when I graduate high school.

BLAKE

"This look is a facade. It's protected me for a while. I fit into their expectations, I'm not outed, and I can coast until I'm out of this shit hole. My 'ideal look' involves a shaved head, watercolor tattoos, body hair, and androgynous attire. I've been socialized to look 'cute' and through positive reinforcement when I dress up, I allow myself to slip back into this femme look when I 'dress up." I don't know how to make the leap from woman to gender-less or whatever I am. If I could dress how I wanted, I'd have friends who get me. They'd probably think like me — or at least a lot more like me than my Christian cheerleader friends. People write me off and reject me immediately, writing me off as superficial, fake, and 'bitchy."

Homecoming is going to solidify this image even further. My mom bought me a tight black dress with ruffles and rhinestones, red high heels, and a giant gemstone-covered head-band for my hair. The headband gives me a headache and so does this getup.

Chapter 2

☿ Gender and Identity ♀

Navigating the world of gender identity is becoming increasingly complex as people become more aware that there are realities beyond the binary of girl/ boy and woman/man. This chapter provides support on how to figure out yourself and other people in a complex world of gender-based expectations around expression, life choices, relationship models, and more.

NOTE: Some parts of this chapter talk about sexual anatomy, which is explained in detail in Chapter 4. If you aren't sure about the biology when it comes up, take a peek two chapters ahead.

Gender + Identity = You

The ideas of gender and identity are about who you feel like on the inside. They aren't things that someone else can tell you about your-self—and they aren't things that you are required to tell anyone else. Often, people will make assumptions about your gender and identity. Those assumptions can be useful, harmful, or neutral—it depends on your relationship with the person making the assumptions, what kinds of assumptions they are making, and how aware they are of their as-sumptions.

Let's dive into the idea of gender. Many gender identity words may be new for some people, so before we can talk about how you feel about your gender identity and how you relate to other people in healthy ways depending on, or regardless of, your gender identity, we need to define the words we'll be using.

Gender: A cultural idea about who you are that is made up of iden-tity, expression, and biology.

Gender identity: Who you think you are (including woman, man, and many other, less culturally common words).

Gender expression: The way you express who you are (including feminine, masculine, androgynous, many other, less culturally common words).

Biology: The physical constructs that humans have culturally associated with gender, often considered to be a person's sex (including female, male, intersex, and a few other, less culturally common words).

The thing to know about these different ways of experiencing, understanding, and expressing gender, is that they aren't either-or. Each person can have a whole lot of all of them, very little of any of them, or some other potential mix-and-match of traits and identities. Let's take a look at these constructs on an adorable picture of a cookie:

The Genderbread Person[1]

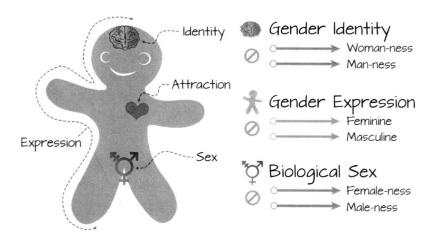

---

[1]It's even cuter in color, which you can see here: http://itspronouncedmetrosexual.com/2015/03/the-genderbread-person-v3/

Most of the people who are reading this book, which is written for teen girls, will identify as more woman than man on the gender identity spectrum above. But there might be other kinds of people reading this book, too. Maybe you're a person who identifies with man-ness, but your family and peers think that you identify with woman-ness because of your biology. Or maybe you're a person who doesn't identify with either woman-ness or man-ness. Regardless of how you or anyone else identifies, gender identity is something that exists inside you that can't be seen from the outside unless you make it apparent. Sometimes people choose to make their gender identity apparent, by wearing a dress, for example, and sometimes it's unintentional, like the way that they walk.

The ways that people make their gender identity known is through their gender expression. Gender expression, like clothing choices and the ways that we hold and move our bodies, are cultural constructs. That means each culture decides what gender expressions typically match with which biological sexes. Cultures change these things over time and they are sometimes very different between cultures. For example, in the United States, pink used to be considered a good color for boys but now it's commonly associated with girls.

Many people assume that biological sex is what defines someone's gender identity and gender expression. There's no medical reason to think this, though, so many people are wrong.

Use a pencil to draw stars on where you think you fall on each of the six lines on The Genderbread Person graphic.

 Note: There is another piece to this graphic that's about sexual orientation. Gender is all about an individual person, without considering how they interact with others. Sexual orientation, or sexual identity, is about whom someone interacts or wants to interact with romantically and/or sexually. Before we can dive into who you are/aren't/might be interested in, it's important to take some time to consider yourself on your own, individual terms.

Take a look at the Gender Q's below. Even if you feel like your gender is pretty straightforward, I hope you'll still think about your answers. You may consider aspects of yourself that you haven't thought about before. Considering these questions also will help you understand other people better by thinking about the issues that your friends and peers who don't quite feel certain of their gender might grapple with.

Gender Q's

1. Do you think about yourself growing up to be a woman? Why or why not?

2. How do you know your answer to the first question?

3. What are three things you think of about being feminine? What are three things you think of about being masculine?

4. Circle the words from the list you made in question 3 that feel the most authentic to you, personally. Are more of them feminine or masculine, are there equal numbers of both, or not much of either?

5. Does your biology fit into the female or male category? How does your biology impact/interact with your gender identity?

6. If you were to give all of your answers here, anonymously, to someone to read through, do you think they would expect that you identify as a man or a woman or in some other way? Is that the way you identify? Does it matter if people's expectations are in line with how you identify?

It may be interesting, if you want to think more about gender, to pick a person who is different from you (someone famous, maybe) and guess what their answers to the Gender Q's might be. Of course, these would just be made-up assumptions on your part, which, although they may be useful as we learned earlier, they may be completely wrong.

Some girls are encouraged to wear dresses, makeup, and enjoy certain things. Nothing made sense when I was a kid. I knew that if I actually tried on my sister's dresses like I had thought to, I would get yelled at, maybe grounded.

The first time I ever actually wore a dress, I had that same feeling. Am I going to get yelled at? Punished? My parents are supportive of gay people, but this is different. Will they still love me if they find out? Suppressing who I am and was for 20 years has been... difficult, to say the least.

I feel like I missed out on so many classic girl things, too. Like all-girl sleepovers, being asked to prom, wearing dresses to dances. I feel like I had to come to terms with my femaleness on my own, while all my other female friends were able to do it together and help each other out. God, it's so lonely here. Every girl I know has been through all this. No matter how much older I am than them, it's like I'm the little girl looking up to them. I always think "wow, I can't wait to be like her one day."

Our society encourages us to be our own person, which is great, but I can't be my own person in isolation. There's no point to expressing myself if I can't share even a portion of it with the people around me. In a way, it is human nature to express ourselves.

So naturally I had to come out as a transgender girl, even if no one wanted or expected me to.

ERIN

Here are a few more words that are useful to have in your linguistic tool belt when you're talking about gender:

Cisgender: A person whose sex assigned at birth is the same as their gender identity.

Transgender: A person whose sex assigned at birth isn't the same as their gender identity.

Genderqueer or gender nonconforming: A person whose gender identity does not fit easily into a binary system of gender as only male and female.

There is growing awareness of people who are transgender, genderqueer, and gender nonconforming—and that is good for everyone, including people who are cisgender. The connection between gender identity and sex assigned at birth are so deeply ingrained in our cultural belief structure that many cisgender people never go through a period of self-analysis around their gender. In fact, it is common for people who are cisgender to be entirely unaware of their gender identity as distinct and identifiable. The global benefit of becoming aware of gender identity and sex as different is that it moves the culture away from rigid gender roles, which benefits everyone by opening doors and opportunities.

If you are reading this book, I am working from the assumption that either you have a gender identity of girl/woman OR someone else assumes you have a gender identity of girl/woman. Regardless of how or why you are here, you are welcome. The issues of gender and sex are not, sadly, an exclusively personal concern. There are many assumptions and associations that the culture around you makes based on the facts of your biology and your gender expression.

Here are a few things that are important to understand about gender, sex, and identity:

- **You do not have to fit into anyone else's gender box.** Even while knowing words like genderqueer and trans, plenty of people feel that their only options of gender expression are stereotypical. But this isn't true. Even people who are cisgender often flow between different modes of expression and identity, and research has shown that they are emotionally and psychologically healthier for it.

- **Your gender identity and your gender expression are not always the same.** A person's gender identity is internal and is not choice based. Gender expression, on the other hand, is external and is mostly choice. However, just because expression is choice based does not mean that it is either easy or healthy for a person to live expressing their gender differently than their gender identity.

- **Coming out does not always make things better.** This applies to both gender identity and sexual orientation. In the beautiful, accepting world that I dream of, coming out would always make things better. The reality of our world, however, is not always kind to people who come out. Sometimes parents and guardians and those closest to a person are not supportive or loving when that person comes out. Particularly in those situations, it is often safest for a young person to refrain from coming out to their families until they are financially independent. Finding a safe person or two to talk with, if possible, can be sanity-saving.

- **Gender expression and sexual orientation are not one and the same.** There are often assumptions made about a person who expresses themselves in a particularly masculine way ("Must be sexually and romantically interested in girls!") or feminine way ("Must be sexually and romantically interested in boys!"). But gender expression does not make sexual orientation, and nor does sexual orientation make gender expression. To be specific: because a woman prefers short hair and pants does not mean she is romantically or sexually attracted to women.

To understand these particularly hot-button issues, it's important to consider the ways that culture puts its finger on the gender button and the ways that it restricts relationships, including heterosexual, gay, lesbian, and all other iterations of love and sex.

Gender + Relationships + Culture = ?

When many people look at you, they will make assumptions about who you are and what sorts of things you enjoy. We talked about this in Chapter 1. It is the nature of human culture to make assumptions as a short cut. Sometimes this serves us well and sometimes it doesn't.

There may be one or two people who fit into narrow gender roles, but I'm sure that you know women who have masculine traits and men who have feminine traits. In fact, most of the people you know probably live far outside of narrow gender based stereotypes, regardless of their gender identities. There has been good, hard, cultural work done in the United States to move many Americans beyond gender-role assumptions. We are generally still aware of them, but many people are also aware that any one individual person is likely to exist and experience life outside of strict gender roles.

However, gender-based assumptions about relationships are often still intact. These are destructive assumptions about men being providers and women caring for the home and family. And if those assumptions don't hold, or the relationship doesn't include a man and woman, there remains an association that the person who earns more money will also be the one to do the yard work and take out the trash, and the person who earns less money will do more of the cleaning. In other words, even when biological sex doesn't clearly translate into which household chores are "blue" and which are "pink," gender expression often takes its place to rigidly assign gender roles.

The rigidity of relationship assumptions that are based in gender aren't easy to figure out among teenage couples. But nevertheless, gender assumptions do impact high school relationships, mostly around decisions about sex, and mostly due to misinformation about humanity's origins. The origin story goes like this:

I am so, SO freaking mad right now!! we just got home from an Indian wedding where I saw something great - a female Hindu priest who officiated the whole ceremony. I thought it was the coolest thing in the whole world, since all of my life I've only ever seen male priests, and I didn't even know that Brahmin women were ever allowed to be priests! But what completely got my blood boiling was an Aunty that I was talking to said it was "disgusting" and "completely against our culture" to have a female priest. When I asked her why, her reasoning was that women have periods, and that is considered "unclean", so how could an "unclean" person possibly be officiating a marriage?

I was stunned when I heard this - and that too from another woman!! If she wasn't an elderly lady, I would have screwed all sense of "respect" and societal norms and straight up asked her if she considered herself unclean too. Instead, I asked her what her thoughts were on pooping. Yup, you heard right, pooping. She giggled like a school girl and said that poop is unclean

ANJALI

too, "obviously". So I asked her how come male priests aren't cosidered dirty or unclean, when they poop every. single. day? The look on her face was priceless. This wonderful Aunty followed up my question by opening and closing her mouth several times like a foolish, silk-clad goldfish, before hurriedly pretending that someone called her name and walking away.

This. This ridiculous shit is something that I absolutely cannot deal with. The huge taboo around menstruation, even though its a simple biological phenomenon and without which having children wouldn't be possible. The stigma around sex, and especially female pleasure — a stigma that supersedes geographical boundaries and is very much present here in the much more "liberal" country of America as well. I used to think that things were _so_ different between India and America when it came to women's rights, feminism, and sex, but in reality, the stigmas are very much the same, perhaps only the societal and ~~cultural~~ cultural contexts are different.

Gender norms are so very present in both countries, and so very toxic and harmful to ALL genders, not just to women. To this day, you can't go a day in the USA without hearing "oh that's so gay" if a man does something that society deems feminine. You can't go a day without a woman being called "butch" or a "Lesbo" if she likes beer and doesn't conform to female gender norms. In India, according to the outdated gender roles, women are meant to be housewives whose only job is producing children and pleasing her husband sexually and fulfilling every need. It's ridiculous and shameful and limiting, and needs to stop. That's not to say that progress and change hasn't come about in both countries, but to this day there isn't nearly enough of it because gender norms and roles are so deeply rooted within us that it's nearly impossible to fight them off.

Whew, that was quite a rant! I can go on for AGES about this shit to be honest. My blood boils whenever I meet small-minded people like this Aunty, and it honestly just gives me more fuel to fight against these deep-set prejudices (and people like this Aunty who spread it) and hopefully change the world, a bit at a time. Equality FTW!

When we were first humans, living as nomads and hunters and gatherers, men were able to continue their genetic lineage the most effectively by having many women birth their babies. Women were able to continue their genetic lineage most effectively by having one man commit to her and their babies exclusively. And so, men want to have sex with as many women as possible, while women want to have a monogamous relationship with just one man. Thus, men and women are always in relationship conflict.

Our contemporary culture says that this story and theory applies to all humans: Men still want to have lots of sex partners and women still want just one. This is where we get the "boys-will-be-boys" tendency to overlook boys who sleep around while we condemn girls who want more than one partner. This origin story also supports the idea that families should live in two parent households that are independent from other families. While actual information on the anthropological origins of humans is cloudy due to the lack of written history, there's not a lot of biological or psychological evidence to support this idea of boys and girls. Rather than the separation of individual family units that this idea represents, humans were more likely bonded in groups where we birthed and raised our families in communities rather than in nuclear families of one man, one woman, and their children. Rather than any individual, like a mother, relying solely on another individual, like a father, the larger community relied on itself and supported itself. What this means about individual relationships and about men and women and how they are *supposed* to interact isn't immediately clear. But it does mean that it's unlikely that men have a genetic predisposition to multiple partners or that women have a genetic predisposition to monogamy.

And on to the Family

NOTE: In this and future sections where we talk about parents, I use that word, "parent," to refer to a wide range of adults who may act as a parent for you. Some adults who serve in a parent role might actually be your grandparent, sibling, aunt or uncle, cousin, teacher, minister, priest, foster parent, therapist, coach, or one of many other adults that young people have in their lives. What

I mean by parents are the adult(s) who helped to raise you, who help support you financially and emotionally, and who have and may continue to influence the ways that you think about the world.

The family we come from guides our initial understanding of gender, relationships, culture, and identity. The ways that our parents interact with their own gender, with each other's genders, with the genders of our siblings and friends, and the way they treat us based on our gender all matter. Here are a few of the ways this matters (see if you can guess if the parent thinks the child is a boy or a girl based on cultural stereotypes.):

- A baby's room is decorated in pink with princesses.
- A 3-year-old is told to toughen up when they cry from falling in the street.
- A 6-year-old is encouraged in science and Legos.
- A 9-year-old is enrolled in ballet and gymnastics.
- A 13-year-old is told that they look inappropriate in a tank top and shorts.
- A 15-year-old is given a white ice-skate Christmas tree ornament decorated with silver glitter and feathers.
- A 17-year-old changes shirts in a parking lot and the parent doesn't notice or mention it.
- A 19-year-old gets a high-five from their father when they start dating a 25-year-old.

How do we know which gender child these parents were likely interacting with? (In order, these children are most likely: girl, boy, boy, girl, girl, girl, boy, and boy.) Why is it easy to guess whether a parent will encourage a boy or a girl in science and Legos? These are cultural messages, but more to the point, they are family messages and family values. These parents aren't actively working to restrict their children's choices. Rather, these parents are making assumptions that their children will follow culturally assigned gender roles. The reality is that some children will follow all of them, some children won't follow any of them, and most children will follow some and not others. Cultural and parental assumptions about gender make their way into children's heads early—most 3-year-olds can tell you whether they are more likely to see a female or male nurse. Of course, by the time those 3-year-olds have grown into teenagers, they're unsurprised by a nurse who is a man, but they probably have other, more hidden assumptions about gender that will influence the ways that they interact with their peers and their sexual and romantic partners. These gender lessons run deep. So while teenagers can, and should, move beyond their parents' assumptions, it's hard for anyone to shift past their childhood conceptions of things like gender, race, religion, age, and money, without some serious introspection.

It is important to consider your parents' perspectives about gender and whether or not you agree with them. It's also important to consider your romantic and sexual partner's parents' perspectives on gender, because they will have influenced your partner's perspectives, whether they agree with them or not. If you're spending a lot of time with someone whose parents think that a woman should stay home and a man should earn lots of money to support his family—how does that align with your perspective? Has your partner considered the question? If you're dating someone, and you haven't talked much about gender roles in relationships, you might both benefit from asking each other the Gender+Relationship Q's on the next two pages.

But What About the Lesbians?

Wouldn't it be nice if lesbians were able to break free of all gender assumptions? After all, if there are two women in a relationship, someone still has to do the "blue" jobs like taking out the trash—but why would those jobs be distributed to only one person? Why would the other person only do the "pink" jobs? It isn't immediately clear why in same-sex relationships, gender roles would be assigned according to how they are assumed to work in heterosexual relationships. But, in fact, this is often exactly what happens, especially in communities where rigid gender stereotypes are common among heterosexual couples.

Being aware that same-gender relationships still have issues with the cultural assumptions of gender roles and gender stereotypes is important. It is too often the case that one person will pick up the masculine roles while the other person picks up the feminine roles, without attention or discussion. Dividing roles along those lines might or might not be good for the relationship. Without considering whether gender roles are negatively impacting the relationship dynamics, a same-sex couple can fall into negative patterns even more easily than a heterosexual couple. There are growing conversations around feminism and gender-role dynamics that help to expand dialogue in female-male couples, but not in female-female couples. It is important that all couples, regardless of their predominant sexual and romantic attraction pattern, consider the following questions:

Gender + Relationship Q's

1. Write out a list of things that you would expect a boy your age to do in a relationship and a list of things you would expect a girl your age to do in a relationship.

2. If you had to pick just one of these roles to play, which would it be? Would being in that role feel good or restrictive or something else?

3. How would you feel if your partner chose the role that you did not choose? How would you feel if your partner chose the same role that you chose?

4. Do you have one parent who tends toward a gender role and another parent who tends toward the other?

5. When you consider your friends and peers, do they tend to partner in ways where one of them usually takes on one of these roles and the other usually takes on the other? Why do you think that might or might not be?

6. How easy or difficult do you think it might be to break out of gender roles?

Additional Resources

What if you need more information about gender? Here are some great resources:

📖 *The Social Justice Advocate's Handbook: A Guide to Gender* by Sam Killermann

💻 TransWhat? A Guide Towards Allyship (http://www.transwhat.org)

What if you need help thinking about your own gender identity? These are some resources that can help:

💻 Gender Spectrum (https://www.genderspectrum.org)

📖 *The Gender Quest Workbook: A Guide for Teens and Young Adults Exploring Gender Identity* by Rylan Jay Testa, Deborah Coolhart, and Jayme Peta

📖 *My Gender Workbook: How to Become a Real Man, a Real Woman, the Real You, or Something Else Entirely* by Kate Bornstein

E. and I went dancing at a club last night. we were kissing and dancing and it was super romantical and magic. we were at a really big dance club in Austin and I was really excited to be dancing with her. She's beautiful, intelligent, and witty. She and I were both wearing really sexy outfits and we danced and laughed all night. She's the first femme I've dated, so it's interesting to both compliment her outfit (as in you look hot and I want that outfit.)

We were grinding and kissing and these guys in polos approached us, swarming us, and splitting us up quickly. one grabbed my arm and one pulled E by her shoulder. They split us up and began swiftly grinding. I turned around and said no, thank you, but I'm not interested in dancing. She did the same and they attempted to dance with us again. "Come on—" one said. "No dude. I don't want to dance with you" I replied back. "Why not?" he asked. "Because I'm here with my girlfriend and this is a date."

They laughed. "No you're not," they said. "yes, we are. Go away." They laughed again. "If you're together, then prove it. Make out." I told them we'd make out if they did first. They made gagging noises, laughed some more, turned to what seemed to be two friends and began dancing with them.

When I'm seeing a butch person or a man or I'm presenting masculine, I'm infrequently hit on, but for some reason, with E, we are constantly hit on.

BLAKE

I've learned to be a woman and I don't like the way I'm treated when I look more "womanly." I have learned to act like a woman, present as a woman, and consistently acknowledge how much space I feel I am taking up. I wonder what I'd look and be like if I weren't forced into womanhood. I question where the lines of nature/nurture lay for my gender identity and expression.

Chapter 3

Attraction

Young people are questioning their sexual orientation at increasingly high rates. Figuring out sexual orientation now includes not only those who will identify as LGBTQ+, but also those who will identify as primarily or exclusively heterosexual—and that's great! This chapter helps to contextualize and support you as you think about sexual and romantic attractions and then how to communicate those attractions to others.

A Moment on Time + Language

Sexual orientation, and the understanding of it, has expanded so much in the last five or ten years that it's been hard for many people to keep up. There has been an explosion of our understanding of the theoretical structure of sexual orientation and the words that we use to describe it. I don't see any reason for that expansion to slow. For example, even the term "sexual orientation" is shifting to make room for the term "sexual identity." What that means about this book is that by the time you're reading it, the language I've used might be out of date. I hope to present an understanding of sexual orientation/identity as a pattern of romantic and sexual attraction that will hold up to an evolution of the theoretical and linguistic specifics. If the language in this chapter is insufficient, I hope you will pardon the old-sounding words and think about the meanings behind them instead.

Who Are You Attracted to?

That's the first question that people start to ask themselves—or sometimes have answered by listening to their physical and emotional pulls before they even know what it's all about. People have many different answers to the question of whom they are attracted to, but they all start with language, so that's where we will start, too.

It seems fitting that we should start with this common acronym: LGBTQ+.

L (Lesbian): A person who identifies as a woman and is primarily attracted to women.

G (Gay): A person who identifies as a man who is primarily attracted to men. (Can also, in some contexts, include lesbians. Sometimes, although less frequently, people use the word homosexual to mean the same thing.)

B (Bisexual): A person who is attracted to both women and men.

T (Transgender): A person whose sex assigned at birth isn't the same as their gender identity. (See Chapter 2 for more detailed information.)

Q (Queer): A person whose experience of attraction does not fall along a binary understanding of gender.

Q (Questioning): A person who is on the path to discovering their sexual orientation/identity.

+ (Plus): While it doesn't stand for anything specific, the plus sign is important. It indicates inclusivity for people who might otherwise not feel included in the prior terms.

You'll note that this list does not include the term heterosexual. Heterosexual, or straight, refers to a person who identifies as a woman who is primarily attracted to men or a man who is primarily attracted to women. Heterosexuality is the historically dominant sexual identity, and so has been overwhelming represented in music, movies, literature, and more. For many people who identify as heterosexual, thinking about their own sexual orientation and identity has not been top on their priority list. However, the information in this chapter *is* useful for people who identify as straight, particularly given the evolving landscape of sexual identity. As sexual identities become ever more fluid, people of all identities will need to understand themselves in the context of how they relate to the people around them. They may find themselves needing to come out, to clarify who they are and who they are attracted to. They may find themselves sexually or romantically interested in someone with a different primary sexual identity than their own. It's important to learn about yourself and about other people, regardless of your sexual identity.

In other words, the need to understand sexual identity is growing, even for people who are straight. A 2016 study by J. Walter Thompson Intelligence suggested that more than half of all 13- to 20-year-olds identify as non-straight. Instead of following one heterosexual and cisgender path, more people are diving into their own patterns of attractions and identities on a path to more personal understanding. As this trend has taken hold, the LGBTQ+ acronym has continued to grow in fun and exciting ways. Here is an alphabetical list of a few more letters that are now, sometimes, included:

A (Ally): A person who identifies as heterosexual and/or cisgender and is publicly and politically supportive of people who identify otherwise.

A (Androphilic): A person who is attracted to man-ness/masculinity/male-ness.

A (Aromantic): A person who does not experience romantic attraction.

A (Asexual): A person who does not experience sexual attraction.

D (Demisexual): A person who experiences sexual attraction only within the context of a deep emotional connection.

G (Gynephilic): A person who is attracted to woman-ness/femininity/female-ness.

I (Intersex): A person whose biology is not clearly female or male.

K (Kinky): A person whose sexual attractions incorporate activities or kinds of touch that are different than the mainstream culture's assumptions of what is typical.

P (Pansexual): A person who is attracted to people across the gender identity spectrum.

But What About Homophobia and Heterosexism?

What about them, indeed. First, definitions:

Homophobia: Literally means to be afraid of people who have same sex attractions, but most often used to mean being upset by or taking moral issue with people who have same sex attractions. Related terms include biphobia and transphobia, which mean the same thing about bisexual and transgender people.

Heterosexism: The assumption that someone is attracted to people of another gender until told otherwise.

Homophobia is the very ugly underbelly of the sexual orientation conversation. Earlier, I defined sexual orientation and identity as being "about whom someone interacts, or wants to interact, with romantically and/or sexually." Love, romance, and sex are such beautiful, personal things. They don't sound like things that would make people fill their hearts with anger and hate. Yet they do.

Being homophobic is now seen as problematic because a majority of people in the United States are accepting of gay and lesbian identities. However, there are many subcultures within the United States—often, although not always, based in religious communities—that fall somewhere between mildly unwelcoming and aggressively attacking of people who are LGBTQ+. Young people living in these communities can find them stifling, exhausting, crushing, and even deadly. If you live in one of those communities, regardless of your own sexual orientation, know that there is life, breath, support, and love outside of them. LGBTQ+ youth do not need to suffer abuse at the hands of their families and communities. There are resources at the end of this chapter that may provide support for those most in need of it.

Heterosexism is a very different beast than homophobia. Heterosexism is more like a death through a thousand, million paper cuts. Heterosexism is the microaggressions that LGBTQ+ people and their families face through other people's incorrect and limited assumptions. Here are a few examples of what heterosexism looks like:

- Your grandmother asks if you are dating a nice boy. (You're a lesbian.)

- Your school forms ask for both your mother's and your father's contact information. (Your parents are both fathers.)

- Your friend asks you whether you would rather have sex with Hot Boy Celebrity 1 or Hot Boy Celebrity 2. (You're asexual.)

None of these gestures necessarily mean that the asker would be bothered if you told them you were gay—or queer or pansexual or asexual. But they are making assumptions. Over time, those assumptions build up and become a very heavy burden. Here are a few examples of heterosexist assumptions turned into questions or statements:

- How can you be sure you're a lesbian? Have you even tried having sex with a man yet? I mean, you have long hair and stuff, so . . .

- Since you like girls and boys, will you have sex with me and my girlfriend?

- I totally get being a lesbian—boys are so horrible and inconsiderate to date, I think about switching sometimes, too!

Again, these statements aren't deeply homophobic or contributing to active physical violence or discrimination against LGBTQ+ people. But they are based in a problematic understanding of what it means to be LGBTQ+, and they can be emotionally difficult to respond to over and over again, if you identify as LGBTQ+. If you identify as cisgender or heterosexual and you consider yourself an ally, educating people about what it means to be LGBTQ+ is an important part of that role.

Education is the primary hope for people who are contributing to the cultures of homophobia and heterosexism. If you identify as LGBTQ+ and have the time and energy, and you feel that you have the right words to say in response to someone's hateful comments, of course you can talk about it right then and there. But you don't need to feel obligated. It's okay to roll your eyes and move on. Some people feel that educating their close friends and family, but not anyone else, is the best answer for them; some opt for educating regardless of who

3. doesn't really want to date and thinks that sex sounds weird?

4. feels somewhere in between being a girl and a boy with aspects of both, and is attracted to girls?

5. introduces herself as a transgirl who doesn't want a relationship right now, but thinks that boys are cute?

Answers for **Sexual Orientation + Gender Identity Quiz**

1. – 5. However they define themselves.

This answer might seem like a cop-out because it's not really answering the question that you thought was being asked, but it's the answer that should always be given. People identify in many different ways—some of them easy to pinpoint, others less immediately clear—and identities are not for anyone other than the individual to claim. That said, here are my best guesses for how these people *might* identify:

1. Cisgender, pansexual/queer

2. Male, heterosexual

3. Asexual/aromantic

4. Genderqueer, gynephilic

5. Transgender, heterosexual

Additional Resources

What if you need more information about sexual orientation? Here are some great resources to read:

- *Speaking OUT: Queer Youth in Focus* by Rachelle Lee Smith (http://rachelleleesmith.com/speakingout/)

- Black Girl Dangerous (http://blackgirldangerous.org)

- *Queer: The Ultimate LGBT Guide for Teens* by Kathy Belge and Marke Bieschke

- Fenway Health LGBT Helpline & Peer Listening Line (for 25 and under): 800.399.PEER

- Gay, Lesbian, and Straight Education Network (GLSEN) (http://www.glsen.org/)

SO IT WASN'T THE NORMAL B.S. OF A DAY TODAY. IT'S WAS KINDA INTERESTING, IT JUST SUCKS THAT I HAD TO COME HOME TO THIS MISERABLE HOUSEHOLD. ANYWAY, CHRISTINA, AND I KISSED IN THE GIRLS BATHROOM. I NEVER FELT ANYTHING LIKE IT, SHE WAS SO SOFT, HER LIPS TASTED LIKE WARM HONEY AND COCOA BUTTER. KISSING HER FELT SO GOOD AND BAD, I DIDN'T LIKE THAT FEELING AT ALL. IF FELT LIKE _MY_ HEART WAS GETTING HEAVY AND DROPPING TO THE PIT OF MY STOMACH. LIKE THE STING OF A SLAP IN THE FACE GRANDMA LOVED TO GIVE ME REPETITIVELY. HOW COULD SOMETHING SO WRONG FEEL SO GOOD THOUGH? WHENEVER WE'RE TOGETHER SHE MAKES ME FEEL BETTER THAN ANY BOY I EVER CRUSHED ON. AND THAT'S A BIG THING, CAUSE JUST LIKE MY TEACHER IN ELEMENTARY SCHOOL TOLD MY GRANDMOTHER AFTER GETTING CAUGHT WITH A BOY IN THE CLOSET, YOUR GIRL LIKES BOY'S A LITTLE TOO MUCH, YOU BETTER WATCH HER, WHEN HE WAS THE ONE WHO PUSHED INTO ME AND KISSED ME. I REALLY LIKE HER AND I KNOW IT'S WRONG TO LIKE HER. GOD DOESN'T LIKE SIN AND HE WOULD HATE ME AFTER THIS, BUT THEN AGAIN, HE HASN'T SAVED ME OR HELPED ME WHEN I PRAY. I'M SO CONFUSED AND I'M AFRAID TO TELL GRANDMA BECAUSE SHE WILL SURELY BEAT THE SHIT OUT IF ME. I DON'T THINK I'LL EVER UNDERSTAND THIS FEELING I HAVE FOR CHRISTINA. WHAT IF THIS HAPPENS WITH ANOTHER GIRL? WHAT AM I GONNA DO? I WANT HER TO BE MY GIRLFRIEND SO BAD DUDE. I REALLY HOPE THAT THIS KISS WILL HAPPEN AGAIN, IT GAVE ME SO MUCH PEACE. I GUESS A MIRACLE IS GONNA HAVE TO HAPPEN BETWEEN US AND MY FAMILY. OH WELL, I DON'T CARE, I'M GONNA KEEP KISSING HER UNTIL SHE TELLS SHE DOESN'T WANT TO ANYMORE. MY HAPPINESS COUNTS MORE THAN ANYTHING RIGHT?

MARGARET

Chapter 4

Inside and Outside Bodies[1]

This chapter includes a full description of the two most common types of internal and external sexual anatomy, both reproduction- and pleasure-based. Next, this chapter moves past anatomy and physiology to talk about body image. How the body is portrayed, perceived, and received is so important. Feeling warm acceptance toward your own body is a dramatic marker of mental health, and the genitals are a great place to start cultivating that feeling. Descriptions of the anatomy described in this chapter are in the Anatomy Glossary at the end of the book.

Biology

Biology is not the end-all-be-all of sex, but it's a pretty important part of the conversation. Everything that happens for you—sexually and romantically, physically and emotionally—takes place in your body, because that's where you live and spend all of your time. Understanding this container that holds your sexuality, that influences you, that molds your attractions, and that allows you to interact with other people, is a good first step to understanding the rest of the topics in this book.

When discussing sexual biology, people usually talk about two primary expressions of sex—the female and male expressions. A specific set of genes, hormones, and internal and external anatomy are usually associated with each of these categories. However, people with all

---

[1]Co-authored with Jessica Smarr, MPH

Many girls have the genitalia that is usually referred to as the female anatomy. You can see drawings of the female anatomy below and a detail of the vulva and clitoris on the next page. Not everyone who identifies as a girl or a woman will have all of these body parts. Among girls who do have all of these parts, there is a lot of variation in size, shape, color, and more. The drawing is labeled, and you can find descriptions of many of the labeled anatomy parts in the Anatomy Glossary at the end of the book. You might have different words that you use to refer to each of these body parts. Feel free to cross out our words, the standard medical terminology, and write in your own.

There is also a labeled drawing of the male anatomy on the next page, and drawings of both an intact penis and a circumcised penis on page 72. The intact penis has a foreskin, while the foreskin on the circumcised penis was removed.

You may have genitalia that look like these drawings, and you may not. If, for example, you are intersex and it influences what your external genitalia look like, these drawings may not represent you very well at all. In the rest of the chapter, a lot of what is talked about will be lumped into two primary categories—people with vulvas, usually

Female Anatomy

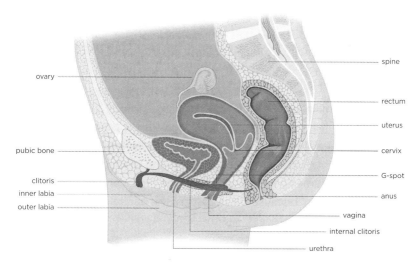

Vulva

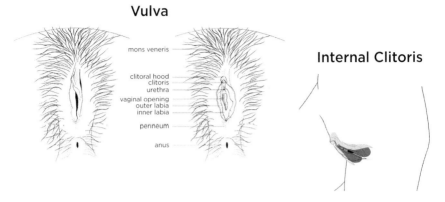

mons veneris

clitoral hood
clitoris
urethra
vaginal opening
outer labia
inner labia

perineum

anus

Internal Clitoris

referred to as female, and people with penises, usually referred to as male. These categories don't adequately represent everyone and their bodies. This is a limitation of language and our ability to communicate, not a limitation of your body.

Secondary Sex Characteristics

Secondary sex characteristics are external features that usually appear during and after puberty and include the enlargement of breasts,

Male Anatomy

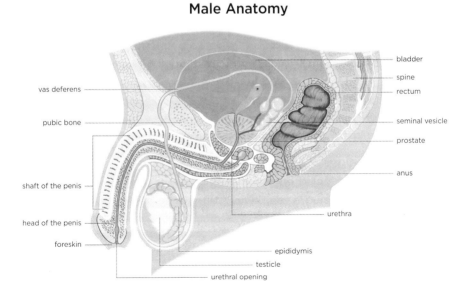

vas deferens

pubic bone

shaft of the penis

head of the penis

foreskin

bladder

spine

rectum

seminal vesicle

prostate

anus

urethra

epididymis

testicle

urethral opening

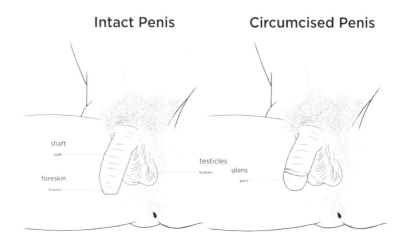

Intact Penis   Circumcised Penis

shaft

testicles

glans

foreskin

growth of hair, and changes in fat distribution. While certain character-istics are thought of as being more common for men or women, there is a lot of variation in when these characteristics develop and what they look like. For example, people who have a vulva usually experi-ence breast growth during puberty that causes them to have larger breasts than people who have a penis. However, breasts vary widely in shape, size, and color for everyone, regardless of genitals.

Literally Everything Else

Fun fact: Every single part of your body can be used to experience or express sexuality! Your brain, for example, might be the most import-ant biological organ when it comes to how you understand the noun *sex* and engage in the verb *sex*. The hormones your brain and several other organs produce affect how you look and feel. The information stored in your brain about things like cultural messages and personal experiences can also play a big role in how you understand and define *sex*—both the noun and the verb.

Your entire nervous system is a crucial player in sexuality. There are nerves throughout your body. When nerve receptors are stimu-lated, they send a message to your brain that can result in a physical sensation. It doesn't even have to be physical stimulation—you could smell something or hear something that results in sexual pleasure!

Consider the following questions about your sex:

Biology Q's

1. How do you feel about your sexual anatomy?

2. What sex was assigned to you at birth? Do you like the way that label feels for you?

The Menstrual Cycle

Now that we've covered the basics of anatomy as it relates to sex, we'll go over a little bit of the function or physiology of sex. This is an introduction to the female reproductive cycle and menstruation. Keep in mind, this section is just an introduction. There are entire books devoted to these topics if you'd like to learn more.

During puberty, people with ovaries and a uterus begin to have menstrual cycles. The menstrual cycle is the process of the uterus preparing for a fertilized egg, or ovum, then shedding the lining of the uterus if an egg is not fertilized. (The process of fertilization will be covered more in Chapter 6, which is all about pregnancy.) When the lining is shed, it exits the body through the vagina. This is what people call menstruation, having a period, or "that time of the month."

The first day of your period is considered the first day of the whole menstrual cycle, mostly because it's the most noticeable part of the cycle. Even though what comes out of your vagina during your period is usually called blood, it's actually made up of uterine tissue, vaginal discharge, and bacteria, in addition to some blood. Variation in color and amount of "blood" is normal from cycle to cycle and from person to person. You may have a heavy flow sometimes and a light flow another time. Your menstrual flow may also be pink, red, brown, or black. All of these colors are normal. While rare, if your menstrual flow is gray, that is cause for concern and a conversation with a primary care provider. You can call your local Planned Parenthood if you aren't sure who else to call. The menstrual phase of the cycle lasts an

Tampons have a string hanging off the bottom so that they can be pulled out of the vagina. Tampons should not be left inside the vagina for more than 8 hours or they could make you sick. Many people start with pads when they begin having their period and, at some point, also use tampons because they allow you to do things like go swimming (pads get water-logged)!

But these aren't your only two options. There are other ways that people manage menstrual flow using reusable and environmentally friendly methods:

- Menstrual cup: This is a cup that is placed inside the vagina around the cervix. It catches the fluid without absorbing it. Every few hours, remove the cup, dump it out, and rinse it. There's no risk of getting sick and you can swim with them in!

- Fabric pads: These look very much like disposable pads, except that you wash and reuse them.

- Period underwear: These are new to the market, but many people think they're fantastic. They are like super absorbent fabric pads that are sewn into your underwear.

- Free bleeding: Some people don't use any products at all. Sometimes people who free bleed only do it when they're at home and can be naked with a towel between their legs. Others do it all of the time.

Finding the right menstrual care product for you and your body is important. Don't feel the need to use whatever your mother or other important adult showed you the first time you had a period. Branch out and explore!

Arousal and Pleasure

We're now at the intersection of sexual biology and the verb *sex*. It's no secret that a lot of people really enjoy engaging in and talking about sexual activity. Think about how many songs have been written about it. Almost all of the songs. Scientists, doctors, and researchers also talk about and research sexual activity, although not nearly enough. There's a lot of disagreement among professionals about why we feel sexual pleasure, what it means physically and emotionally, and how to measure it. In the classic academic model of sexual response, there are four stages: excitement, plateau, orgasm, and resolution. The basic and very informal breakdown is:

- Excitement phase: Your body is getting pumped about what's going on and there are some physical changes, like an increased heart rate.

- Plateau phase: Your body is still excited about what's happening, and there are more physical changes like vaginal wetness or an erect penis.

- Orgasm phase: *Wow!* Your body is really excited! Everything feels amazing! Many exclamation points are probably included!

- Resolution: Things calm back down. If you have a vulva, your body can usually jump right back to one of the earlier stages of the cycle. If you have a penis, you usually have to wait a little longer. This waiting time is called a refractory period.

This model is a nice introduction, but the best part of it may be in the caveats—that this isn't how it works for everyone, and the steps aren't always going to follow each other perfectly every time. Some of these steps might not even happen during sexual activity. That doesn't mean it wasn't awesome or meaningful or pleasurable. Some sexual activity will have lots of orgasms; some won't have any at all. And that is okay. So we're going to talk about sexual activity and pleasure and biology, but we're going to move away from this goal-oriented model and language like "achieving orgasm" and instead talk about experiencing orgasm. There's lots more information about orgasms in Chapter 16.

A lot of sexual activity begins with sexual arousal, which is basically the biological response to something that is sexually exciting. A lot of this pleasurable response has to do with the central nervous system. You can perceive something with any of your five senses and become aroused because of the way your brain interprets information. One of the most common ways to experience sexual pleasure is through touch. There are certain parts of the body that have more nerve receptors and may therefore be sites of greater pleasure. These include genitalia like the clitoris and the glans of the penis and other body parts, like the lips, tongue, or fingers. Each person is unique, however, and everyone is going to enjoy something a little different. If you want to bring someone pleasure and you don't know where their favorite spots are, there is one sure-fire way to find out—ask them! If they're not sure, you can explore together. And if you want to bring yourself pleasure, you don't have to stick to just the genitals; you can explore your whole body! More on masturbation is in Chapter 17.

Washing Your Parts

It's important to treat your body kindly and show it some love. Part of that can be keeping your body, including the genitalia, clean and happy. While this might seem obvious, it's not always, so here are the pieces you might be missing:

Vulval Cleanliness

For individuals with vulvas, I've got good news—your body does a lot of the cleaning for you! You can use just plain water to clean external anatomy, like the labia and the mons veneris (the fatty tissue covering your pubic bone). The vagina can be left to its own devices; there's no need for washing or douching. The vagina likes to maintain an acidic, high pH-environment, which is great for the bacteria that live there. If the pH of the vagina changes, it becomes prone to infections. Vaginal pH can change due to a whole lot of things, including the menstrual cycle, sexual activity, diet, and stress. "Hygiene products," even those marketed toward cleaning the vagina like vaginal douches, actually upset the pH of the vagina and should be avoided. If you decide to use tampons, make sure that they are scent-, color-, and bleach-free, because these things can be problems in the vaginal environment. Some of the bacteria and other organisms that cause infections thrive in moist environments, so you can decrease your risk of infection by wearing underwear made with natural fibers like cotton that can absorb moisture.

It's also important to know that the vaginal and anal environments are pretty different, and have different kinds of bacteria in them. For optimal vaginal health, you should avoid getting any fecal matter in your vagina. You can do that by wiping front to back, rather than back to front, after a bowel movement. Also, if you are engaging in sexual activity or using a sex toy, make sure to thoroughly wash any body parts or objects before moving them between the anus and the vagina.

Infections of the vagina are extremely common. Below are two common types of vaginal infections that are not usually considered sexually transmitted infections, or STIs. While they can be sexually transmitted, that is not the primary method of transmission. More information on STIs is in Chapter 5.

Yeast infection: Approximately 75% of people with a vagina will have a yeast infection at some point in their lives. The fancy name for a yeast infection is vulvovaginal candidiasis, but yeast infection is definitely easier to say. Yeast is always hanging out in the vagina, but it can cause an infection when it grows too much too quickly. If you have a yeast infection, you might experience burning, itchiness, or discharge that looks like cottage cheese. However, some people don't have any symptoms at all. If you do have a yeast infection, there are a lot of options for treatment like home remedies, over-the-counter medications, and prescription medications. If you think you have a yeast infection, ask your health care provider for the best plan of action for you and your body. However, it can be very difficult for some people to access health care providers due to things like time, money, transportation issues, and privacy issues. You can also talk with any pharmacist at a grocery or drug store for recommendations on dealing with a yeast infection.

Bacterial vaginosis: Bacterial vaginosis (BV), a bacterial infection of the vagina, is also very common among people with vulvas. It's caused by an upset in the ratio of "good" bacteria to "bad" bacteria in the vagina. The symptoms of BV are similar to those of a yeast infection. It can change the color, texture, and smell of your vaginal discharge, based in a growing awareness of stigma associated with STD, which, for some reason, isn't as strong with STI, and a need for increased medical accuracy. The term STD was originally an attempt to move away from the stigma and medical inaccuracy associated with the term venereal disease (VD), but over time it gathered its own stigma. Additionally, the word *disease* indicates symptoms, whereas many STDs/STIs do not have any symptoms.

The linguistic shift seems to have gone well: more people are willing to get tested for STIs than they were when they were called STDs, and more people seem to know that they need to get tested even if they aren't experiencing any symptoms. From here forward, I am only going to use the term STI because it is more accurate, and now you know that it means the same thing as STD.

STI Details

There are three categories of STIs: viral, bacterial, and parasitic. Here is a general overview of each.

Viral STIs

Viruses, in general, are not considered to be "alive," and therefore we have no ability to "kill" them. The human body has the ability to rid itself of some viruses, like a cold or the flu, but not others, like HIV. We can, however, treat the symptoms with antiviral medication. Viral STIs include: Hepatitis B, Herpes, HIV, and HPV.

Hepatitis B attacks the liver. The body has a hard time getting rid of toxins when the liver is infected. Hepatitis B can cause flu-like symptoms, jaundice, fever, headaches, or joint aches, but sometimes it has no symptoms. Some people's bodies are able to rid themselves of the infection while other people's bodies are not. There is a vaccination against Hepatitis B.

HSV, or the herpes simplex virus, has an immense amount of stigma that needlessly and problematically goes along with it. HSV can be either an oral or a genital infection. When it is an oral infection, it is typically called cold sores. When it is a genital infection, it is typically called herpes. There are two different groups of HSV infections: Type I and Type II. While Type I is typically oral and Type II is typically genital, they can both exist orally or genitally. Both Type I and Type II are treated the same way, with antiviral drugs that keep HSV outbreaks from happening often and allow them to heal more quickly when they do happen. The symptoms that go with a herpes infection can range from nothing at all, ever, to fairly serious, regular, and painful sore outbreaks. Most people don't have outbreaks that cause them substantial problems.

Herpes is very common! In the United States, one in six people has genital herpes and more than half of all people have oral herpes! This means that a positive herpes test doesn't mean that someone shouldn't ever be sexually active again or that there is no way for them to be safely sexually active or that they should hide their infection from a partner. What it does mean is that care should be taken during an outbreak, and that if the outbreaks are common, they should take antiviral medication.[1]

HIV (human immunodeficiency virus) is more complex than most viruses because it's actually a retrovirus. Let's start with how HIV works: HIV enters T-cells, which protect the body from other infections, and turns them into little HIV factories so that they can't continue to function as a barrier to other infections. When enough T-cells have been turned into HIV factories, the entire immune system is damaged and the body can't fight off even very basic infections like a cold. When the immune system is substantially damaged, the person is diagnosed with AIDS (acquired immunodeficiency syndrome). To summarize: HIV is a virus that is transmitted between people and is the cause of an AIDS diagnosis. You cannot catch or give someone AIDS, only HIV. Here are a few truths about HIV that some people are confused about:

- HIV can only be transmitted through bodily fluids, not casual contact. It cannot be caught from a mosquito.

- Early HIV rarely has symptoms, but as it develops, symptoms can include flu-like feelings, weight loss, tiredness, and diarrhea. If you think you may have been exposed to HIV, you should get tested, even if you aren't experiencing symptoms.

---

[1]For more information specifically about herpes, this article does a really good job talking about the stigma and loneliness that many people who have herpes feel (http://www.theatlantic.com/health/archive/2014/07/the-overblown-stigma-of-genital-herpes/374757/). If it's no longer available, go to https://www.plannedparenthood.org and do a site search for herpes.

you. That doesn't mean that they are a bad person or that they won't get there, it just means they aren't ready yet. Don't let them talk you out of knowing your own value as a sexually healthy young woman.

And a Moment on Disclosure

If you have a positive STI test . . .

- Yes, you have to tell your partner(s) if you realize you have an STI after you have been sexually active with them in a way that can transmit that STI, whether it is through fluid exchange or skin-to-skin contact.

- Yes, you have to tell your past partner(s) if it is possible that they became infected with an STI through their sexual contact with you *or* if it is possible that you became infected through sexual contact with them.

- Yes, you have to tell future partner(s) before you are sexually active with them if you are infected with a virus that your body has not or cannot clear itself of.

None of these things are easy to do, but they are the responsibilities that come with the privilege of being sexually active. Doing this is what it means to care for your own, your partners', and your community's sexual health.

If reaching out to someone to inform them that they may have contracted an STI is so overwhelming to you that you are not going to do it, consider using an STI notification service like https://www.DontSpreadIt.com. This website allows you to inform past or current partners that they may have been exposed to an STI with complete anonymity so that they can get tested and protect themselves.

And a Little More About Condoms

We need to talk about STI prevention (we will talk about pregnancy prevention in the next chapter). There are two general ways that STIs are transmitted: fluid transfer or skin-to-skin contact.

The sexual acts that are typically involved in fluid transfer are vaginal, oral, and anal sex. Manual stimulation, or touching with your hands, can also involve fluid transfer if there are even small cuts on the hands, but it is way less common. The sexual acts that involve skin-to-skin contact include the same three sexual acts as well as manual or hand stimulation and other kinds of kissing and rubbing. The ways to prevent STI transmission are to prevent the fluid transfer and skin-to-skin contact that act as a way for viruses, bacteria, and parasites to move from one person to another. A latex barrier (either a dental dam or a condom) is the most common kind of STI barrier, but there are other options, including a dental dam for oral sex on a vulva and a glove for hand-to-genital touching. There are non-latex options for each of these for people who have latex sensitivities.

One of the primary issues that prevent people from using condoms and other barriers is that they are thought of and talked about as being less pleasurable than not using a barrier during sex. But the good news is that condoms can actually *add* to your sexual pleasure and connection rather than taking it away! The secret comes in two forms: the right fit and lube. Water-based lubricant makes many sexual experiences feel better, and sexual experiences with condoms are no different. The added motion and friction that is possible with lubricant and condoms is a match made in heaven! For everything you've always wanted to know about lubricant and condom fit, Lucky Bloke (https://www.luckybloke.com/) is the best place to go.

Additional Resources

Seductive Delusions: How Everyday People Catch STDs by Jill Grimes, MD

Fact sheets about specific STDs, from the Centers for Disease Control and Prevention (https://www.cdc.gov/std/healthcomm/fact_sheets.htm)

"STIs Aren't a Consequence. They're Inevitable," a TEDx talk by Ella Dawson (https://ellacydawson.wordpress.com/2016/05/11/watch-my-tedx-talk-stis-arent-a-consequence-theyre-inevitable-with-transcript/)

that you can get herpes from skin to skin contact (like oral sex which we definitely didn't use any protection for, both ways) and condoms don't completely protect you from getting it if your partner has it.

But then - I found some more stuff about herpes that made me feel a little bit better. Apparently, herpes is actually incredibly common - as many as 1 in 4 people have it! Isn't that absolutely wild?! It seems like a lot of people can have it and have no idea, because they have no symptoms. And Dr. G. told me that even if I did test positive, herpes is not one of those STDs that will have a huge impact on my life - it will probably stay dormant, and even if I break out with the help of anti-virals I will be alright. That was so relieving to know, especially since I know that ~~with~~ STIs like gonorrhea can affect your fertility if left untreated - which is a huge consequence and very scary!

So I'm feeling a teeny bit better but still freaking out until I get my results back. I'm wondering through all this if I'm feeling this bad, how I must be feeling since he just found this huge news. I'll be seeing him tomorrow and ~~hopefully~~ hopefully we can talk everything out and I can offer him some reassurance from everything that Dr. G told me. For now, I'm going to bed. it's been a long day.

Chapter 6

Pregnancy and Prevention

The reproductive process, including making choices about reproduction, can be an intimidating part of sex. This chapter is packed with information so you never have to make an uninformed decision. Remember, though, that you can't make these decisions alone. You'll need to talk with your partner, and maybe a doctor, too.

Pregnancy: The Good + the Hard + the Scare Tactics

Before we dive deep into the details of pregnancy, let's talk about what pregnancy means. It can be beautiful and it can be scary and it can be what you want and what you don't want—and it can be all of those things at once on a Tuesday afternoon if you're pregnant.

The good things that can come with pregnancy are the excitement of a new little human, full of potential and adorableness. Babies smell good and hold on to your finger. It's easy to love a baby. Babies can bring families together and can help people clarify their goals in life. All of these things are true for parents who are teenagers and parents who are adults.

The hard things that may come with pregnancy are physical, social, emotional, and financial. The hard emotions are difficult to summarize for many reasons, mostly because everyone feels them differently and in ways that are impossible to predict, including both teenagers and adults.

Teenagers are often encouraged to prevent pregnancy at all costs. They're told that if they were to become parents, it would ruin their lives and the lives of their children. But that's not the case. Sure, it is for some. But it's also true for some adults. What matters most is the kind of support network you have, including financial and emotional support and all of the other things. People in their 30s are more likely to have stable networks than people in their teens. But that doesn't mean that anyone should tell you that becoming pregnant and deciding to parent will ruin your life. What's true is that it will change your life. That's all anyone can say for certain, regardless of the parental age.

Pregnancy + Biology

We're going to dive into the details of how the anatomy comes together to produce a pregnancy. The activities outlined here are THE ONLY ONES THAT WILL GET YOU PREGNANT. It may seem extreme for me to have all-caps-ed that information, but sometimes the fear of pregnancy overwhelms people's good sense. Being scared into thinking that other sexual activities will get you pregnant does no one any good. Having the facts is what helps.

The ONLY way to get pregnant is if sperm meet up with an egg.

That's it. That's the only way.

The ONLY way for the sperm to meet up with an egg is if ejaculate is in the vagina.

With the exception, of course, of medical procedures. But for your purposes, until you are actively trying to get pregnant and find that you need alternative ways of doing that, there must be ejaculate in the vagina. On very rare occasions, ejaculate on the surface of the vulva may move deeply enough into the vagina to move up through the vagina, cervix, uterus, and fallopian tubes, but that is very uncommon.

DUDE, ARE YOU FOR REAL? YOU WHERE ALWAYS THE GIRL THAT TOLD YOURSELF WHERE NEVER GONNA GET PREGNANT! WHAT THE HELL IS WRONG WITH YOU?

DIARY, DANIELLE GOT HERSELF PREGNANT. AND NOW SHE'S CRYING AND ASKING ~~CAN~~ ME FOR HELP. WHAT THE FUCK AM I GONNA DO??? I'M JUST 13, I AIN'T GOT NO CRIB... I DON'T EVEN HAVE LUNCH MONEY FROM TIME TO TIME, I STILL GOT AN OVERDUE BALANCE OF $20.34 ON MY LUNCH ACCOUNT. I CAN'T IMAGINE PAYING FOR ANOTHER ME. I JUST UNDERSTAND THE CONCEPT OF IF YOU'RE IN LOVE WITH A GUY, YOU HAVE TO NOT PROTECT YOURSELF. WHAT'S REALLY UP WITH THAT? WHY DO ALWAYS USE THE EXCUSE "WELL BABE IF YOU LOVE ME, WHY DO WE HAVE TO USE A CONDOM? SIR, WE'RE WEARING A CONDOM BECAUSE I LOVE YOU, BUT YOU SO FOCUSED ON HITTING IT RAW, UNLESS YOU WANT THE GIFT THAT KEEPS ON GIVING! HONESTLY, I'M AFRAID OF GETTING PREG- NANT IF I'M NOT READY. AS SOON AS I HEARD HER SAY THOSE WORDS SLIP OUT OF HER MOUTH, I DECIDED TO MAKE AN APPOINTMENT TO GET THE NUVA-RING. I LOVE MY BOYFRIEND BUT I LOVE ME MORE, AND MY OVARIES AS WELL. I WAS THINKING ABOUT GETTING CONTRACEPTION ANYWAY, SEEING AS MY BODY LIKES TO HAVE A MAYWEATHER VS. PACQUIAO FIGHT EVERY MONTH AND I CAN'T FUNCTION, SO THIS WOULD BE A GREAT OPPORTUNITY. AND OF COURSE MY BOYFRIEND DOESN'T MIND SO I CAN'T WAIT FOR MY APPOINTMENT.

MARGARET

But I've gotten ahead of myself. Here are the steps that lead to the overwhelming majority of pregnancies:

1. A penis is inserted into a vagina.

2. After continued sexual contact and arousal, there is orgasm and ejaculation from the penis, which includes sperm (usually 200–250 million sperm!).

3. The ejaculate pools in the vagina and becomes somewhat sticky, keeping it all together.

4. The sperm make their way up the cervix, into the uterus, and down the fallopian tubes, where they will hang out and wait to see if an egg, also known as an ovum, is released from the ovary. The sperm live for about a week, which means that even if you have unprotected sex on your period, it's possible for a pregnancy to begin a week later.

5. From this point, there are two potential outcomes: 1) an ovum is not released or 2) an ovum is released. Option 1 is pretty simple, so I'll clear that up now. The sperm live for about a week in the fallopian tubes and then disintegrate. Eventually the uterus realizes that a fertilized ovum will not be appearing and sheds the lining. Option 2 includes much more, so please continue on:

6. The one-cell ovum is released from the ovary and upon entering the fallopian tube it meets a small handful of one-cell sperm, far fewer than were initially released. Perhaps only 25–30 of them total make it to the fallopian tubes. One of the sperm penetrates the external barrier of the ovum, or perhaps the external barrier of the ovum opens to let one of the sperm in. The exact process isn't fully understood yet.

7. The one-cell sperm and the one-cell ovum combine to form another one-cell fertilized ovum that begins to divide into two, then four, then eight, and then sixteen cells. As it divides, it moves down the fallopian tubes into the uterus.

8. The uterine lining has been building up to prepare for a fertilized ovum. Where the fertilized ovum lands in the uterus is where it will attach and where the placenta will form.

Ideally, much more is involved in the process, like sexual pleasure and mutual respect. But we're staying focused on the pregnancy part here. More about good sex will come in later chapters.

The pregnancy continues from there. The details of pregnancy are far too extensive to be contained in this book, but here are a few interesting facts:

- The placenta forms a barrier between the pregnant person's blood and the embryo's blood. This is how a birth parent can have a different blood type than their offspring. The placenta grows anew with each pregnancy and is birthed after the baby. It is the only human organ that is grown and discarded.

- While pregnancy is usually thought of as being nine months long, it's actually forty weeks, which is a little more than nine months and a little less than ten months.

- The first twelve weeks of pregnancy are considered the first trimester, and this is when many of the major systems like the brain and heart and spinal cord are formed. Damage done to a fetus during this trimester is typically far more devastating than damage done later in the pregnancy because it is to the most basic and necessary parts of a human's anatomy.

- Access to the ovum is *only* possible through the cervix and the uterus. There's no other way for pregnancy to occur.

If you're interested in learning more about pregnancy and childbirth, there are resources listed at the end of this chapter.

Pregnancy + Options

If you find yourself pregnant, or one of your friends finds themselves pregnant, there are a few options that are available to you. The reality is that making a decision about these options is a pressing matter. This is one of those moments in time when ignoring the problem compounds it. Once a pregnancy begins, the clock is running, and honoring and respecting that process is the most responsible, respectful thing to do. If you aren't at all prepared to consider a potential pregnancy, then it's best to not have penile-vaginal intercourse. Even reliable birth control methods can fail, although using two different methods of birth control at the same time, correctly and reliably, is incredibly effective. Nevertheless, ignoring the potential for pregnancy with penile-vaginal intercourse means you might be unprepared for taking responsibility in the event that pregnancy does happen. While I hope that none of you are faced with the decision that an unplanned pregnancy requires of you, I want you to be prepared. So, here are your options:

- Terminating the pregnancy

- Continuing the pregnancy and parenting

- Continuing the pregnancy and finding adoptive parents

It is both very simple and very complex. It is simple to list the options and sometimes simple to decide among them. It is often complex for teens who were not planning a pregnancy to decide among them. Here are a few things you need to know, for each of the decisions:

Terminating the Pregnancy

This is, obviously, the most time-pressured choice. Should you decide to move forward with a termination, also called an abortion, you will need to make that choice within a few weeks of finding out that you are pregnant. Most people don't know that they are pregnant until they are at least four to six weeks along, and maybe even longer if they aren't expecting to be pregnant. Many states restrict abortions to the first 20 weeks of pregnancy, so the decision cannot be ignored.

People have very different feelings about terminating their pregnancy. Here are some facts and statistics about people who terminate a pregnancy:

- Some are clear that a termination is the right choice for them.

- Others think that an abortion is the right decision but are nervous about abortions in general.

- Most of the people who have abortions are in their 20s and already have a child.

- Many people who have abortions are religious. Twenty-four percent of people who terminate a pregnancy identify as Catholic.

Terminating a pregnancy is a decision that is legal and just and sometimes the right thing to do.

Here are some useful things to know about abortion if you're thinking about terminating a pregnancy and you're worried about it[1].

- One out of every 3 women in the United States will have an abortion in their lifetime. **You are not alone.** (http://www.1in3campaign.org/)

- Abortions have been happening since at least 3000 BC. **You are not alone.** (http://www.4000yearsforchoice.com/pages/timeline)

- There is information you can read online to get the facts about what a termination entails. **You are not alone.** (http://www.scarleteen .com/article/bodies/all_about_abortion)

- There are health clinics and chat rooms to get information and help if you are considering having an abortion. **You are not alone.** (https://www.plannedparenthood.org/learn/abortion)

Abortion is highly politicized and may be emotional. There are many myths about abortion in US culture, like that it prevents future pregnancies. These myths work to stigmatize women who choose to terminate a pregnancy. While some people consider abortion to be a medical procedure removing a cluster of cells from the body, others consider it killing a baby. While most people think that access to safe and legal abortions in the United States is an important legal right,

---

[1] If any of these links are broken or out of date, please accept my apologies. Both PlannedParenthood .org and Scarleteen.com are safe and informative websites to search for resources and information on abortion.

other people in their life who care about them and whose thoughts and opinions they respect. Talking with other people allows a diverse range of thoughts and reactions that can help in making the decision. If you don't have anyone close enough to talk with, or just want to talk with someone who isn't involved, you can call Talkline: 1-888-493-0092 (http://yourbackline.org).

Above all, listen to the voice inside you. Trust that voice.

Pregnancy + Prevention

We are just now getting to the prevention piece—the piece that sexually active teenagers usually think about and rely on the most! As we have done so often, let's start with language:

Contraception: A combination of *contra* (which means against) and *ception* (a shortened form of conception, which means the very beginning of something and in this case, the moment when you become pregnant), it means to work against conception or against pregnancy.

There are two primary kinds of contraception: barrier methods and hormonal methods. Barrier methods provide a physical block between the sperm and the ovum. Hormonal methods create a shift in the female body that reduces the likelihood of a pregnancy occurring through a number of changes, including the ovaries no longer producing fertile ova (eggs). Two additional contraceptive methods are surgical and behavioral.

Here are some general guidelines to get you started. For more information, see the Additional Resources at the end of the chapter:

Barrier Methods

Barrier methods include condoms, the most accessible and common kind of contraceptive. There are two kinds of condoms: external, often referred to as male condoms, and internal, often referred to as female condoms. Condoms prevent STI transmission in addition to preventing pregnancy. While many external condoms are made out of latex, there are a variety of latex-free options for people with problematic latex reactions or who just prefer other materials. Internal condoms are not made from latex. For more information on STI prevention, see Chapter 5.

The other kinds of barrier contraceptives (the sponge, diaphragm, and cervical cap) are less commonly used because they are harder to get and use correctly. There is also a barrier intrauterine device (IUD). As the name suggests, it's a small device that's inserted into the uterus.

The downsides of barrier methods, broadly speaking, are that they must be used without error every single time that penile-vaginal inter-course takes place, and some people feel that they are a barrier not only to sperm but also to emotional and physical closeness during sex. The upsides of barrier methods, broadly speaking, are that they do not influence anyone's hormonal or emotional balance, they are easy to stop and start, and that one these methods—condoms—are cheap and easily obtainable. Condoms are distributed for free in many places, including the Planned Parenthood closest to you.

 Note: There are a few contraceptive methods making their way through the FDA approval process that have the potential to really shake up the whole industry. One of those is Vaselgel, a gel that is injected into the vas deferens. It is easily reversible with another injection, costs less than $10, lasts for a decade, and has no known side effects! So if you're reading this after 2018, either Vaselgel will have changed everything about how we think about contraception or it will be an adorable little footnote in the annals of contraceptive history. Isn't being on the cutting edge of science fun?

Hormonal Methods

Hormonal contraception introduces a balance of estrogen and pro-gestin in the body. The balance of hormones depends on the specific contraceptive—some have more of one or the other and some have only one hormone. There are a lot of different ways that hormonal contraceptives get the hormones into the body, including the pill, IUD, implant, ring, and shot. Some people's bodies are more receptive to one kind of hormonal contraceptive rather than another.

There is one kind of hormonal contraception that is different than the others: emergency contraception (also sometimes called the morning-after pill or Plan B). This is a single dose pill that has a very

A Note on Self-Compassion

Relationships are hard: being in them, talking about them, figuring out what you want from them. All hard.

As we talked about in Chapter 4, self-compassion can support you when things get hard. It's pretty much just what it sounds like: Treat yourself with the same kind of compassion with which you would treat a friend. How would you support a friend who was sad or in pain? When you are feeling low, care for yourself with kindness and love.

The ideas behind self-compassion are that instead of working toward self-esteem, or thinking that we are particularly good at something, we should work toward self-compassion, or being kind to ourselves. It can make a world of difference. (Find out more about self-compassion here: http://self-compassion.org/)

Chapter 7

Decision Making

Deciding what you want is the first step to getting what you want, whether that is a sexual or romantic connection or strawberries for breakfast. Before you can decide what you want, though, you must trust your inner voice, your intuition, and your insights. This chapter is designed to support you in listening to the voice inside, which will make it easier to make decisions about relationships and sexuality. This chapter is written in support of your ability to know yourself and to trust in that knowledge.

From Decisions, Everything Else Flows

Knowing what you want is the first step to making what you want happen. This is as true in love, sex, and romance as it is in educational goals, friendship, and getting the job of your dreams. None of which come easily if you don't know that you want them. Similarly, it's harder to avoid something that you *don't* want if you don't know that you don't want it.

I know that sounds a little circular. If you really do want strawberries for breakfast, but you haven't thought about it much, it's unlikely that you'll end up with strawberries for breakfast. It also means that if you don't want bacon, but you haven't considered bacon as a possibility, you may end up eating it reluctantly if someone gives it to you.

Knowing what you want isn't the only step to getting what you want, but it is the first step. There are many ways to make decisions, like flipping a coin or making a list or asking someone else to tell you what you should do, and there are all kinds of decisions that need to be made around sexual activity, self-disclosure, and more. Let's start with the kinds of decisions you'll probably be faced with.

What Kinds of Decisions Will I Have to Make? Or Have I Already Made?

Will you or won't you . . . ? Do you want to or do you not want to . . . ? This is probably how you will begin the decision-making process for lots of things that will come up, including sex, sexuality, romance, and identity. Below are examples of how these questions may end.

Possible Sexual Decisions

Do I want to . . . ?:

- Flirt with someone

- Kiss someone

- Touch someone

- Have someone touch me

- Go on a date

- Dance with someone

- Text someone

- Respond to someone else's text

- Tell someone I love them

- Tell someone to stop touching me

- Have oral sex with someone

- Have vaginal sex with someone

- Have anal sex with someone

- Pick a birth control method

- Get tested for STIs

- Ask a current/future partner to get tested for STIs

- Try to get pregnant/get my partner pregnant

- Tell someone my gender identity

- Tell someone my sexual orientation

- Watch porn

- Take a sexy picture of myself

• Send someone a sexy picture of myself

. . . and So. Many. More. Things.

Decision making is an ongoing, evolving process that can shift quickly, and that can be fun and sexy, stressful and scary, or many other things in between. Some people feel the fun of decision making more than the stress; they focus on the possibilities for good. Some people feel the stress of decision making more than the fun; they focus on the possibilities for heartbreak and negative life consequences.

Incorporating a little of both fun and stress into your decision-making process is ideal, because sexuality is both fun and life changing. You will need to consider both the good (fun) and the difficult (stressful) to make responsible sexual decisions. Below are a few questions to consider about your own process of decision making.

Decision-Making Q's

1. What sexual decisions, if any, have you made already? What sexual decisions do you see in your future?

2. In the list of Possible Sexual Decisions on pp. 130–131, are there any questions that you haven't yet been faced with? Are there any that you don't see yourself facing in the future?

3. Are there decisions that aren't listed that you think you will be faced with? What are they?

4. When you think about sex and sexuality, what are the most important factors affecting your decision? Do you consider your family's perspective? How strong your feelings are for the other person? How that person has treated you in front of their friends? Your religious beliefs?

Decision by System

There are so many different systematic ways to make decisions, and everyone seems to have a theory about the best one. Here are a few.

I. The most basic systematic decision-making process is to make a list of the pros and cons that each decision would bring. Choose the option that has the most pros and the fewest cons.

II. Another pretty simple approach is to answer the following questions, in the following order:

    a. What are the facts?

    b. How do you feel about the facts?

    c. Where do you see the pros, cons, and maybe even options you hadn't thought of yet?

    d. Who will be affected and how?

    You may notice that this builds on to the first system.

III. The third option is a much more complex decision-making process that builds on both of the first two.

Identify the problem or the question.

Figure out how you're going to make the decision. What factors are going to be the most important? (What you want? What advice your parents/religion/friends would give you? What is sexually or emotionally safe? What is best for your future? Some combination of these questions?)

Based on the factors you're using to make your

decision, what matters the most (honesty, sexual pleasure, emotional connection, long-term impact)?

Come up with all of the possible solutions/answers to the problem/question.

Figure out how well each of the solutions/answers addresses your initial question based on your most important factors and the things that matter the most.

Choose the best solution/answer.

Put the solution/answer into practice.

Think about whether the solution/answer helped you consciously consider future decision-making processes.

There are more ways of systematically making decisions—too many to list here. If you want to see more, do a search for "decision-making model" and read through a few of the results that come up.

Pros: Allows what you want, from a place of rational thinking, so that you are not making important decisions without critical consideration.

Cons: The responsibility is yours if you make the wrong decision; you may over-think the process and forget to listen to your gut, or that voice deep inside you.

Making-Decision Q's

1. How have you made decisions about sex and sexuality in the past?

2. Have you felt good about some decisions and less good about other decisions? If so, why?

3. Compare the decisions you felt good about and the decisions you felt bad about. What was different about them?

A Few More Thoughts on Decision Making

All of the approaches to decision making are good under certain situations, even default. For example, when you're visiting a friend's house, it's nice if you are able to decide what you're going to eat for dinner by default: whatever it is that they serve you. If you're asked if you prefer water or soda to drink, deciding by gut is best. If you're deciding what career you want to undertake, a systematic approach is best. This is not to say that people always use the best approach or that sometimes following your gut even with a big decision can't end well.

In the Additional Resources list at the end of this chapter, there is a link to a TED talk about decision making. Among many other valuable insights, the presenter says, "We unwittingly assume that values like justice, beauty, kindness, are akin to scientific quantities like length, mass, and weight." What she means by this is that we can't always know, scientifically and without a doubt, the answer to a question or the solution to a problem. While it might be easier if we could know all of the answers and solutions, it would also mean that our world was boring and predictable. Much of the beauty in life comes from the unexpected and unplanned. Making decisions by systematic thought can't be done without acknowledging the raw beauty in the unexpected moments. Integrate a balance, try to find a system that encourages you to listen to your gut while being systematic in the times that matters most.

What Next?

Decision making does not equal action taking, nor does it mean that you get what you want. This is particularly true when it comes to sexual activities, because they usually involve another person. So after you make a decision, you are only at the very beginning of the process. After you've figured out what you want, you have to talk or interact with the other person to see if it's what they want too.

Additional Resources

- "How to Make Hard Choices," a TED talk by Ruth Chang (https://www.ted.com/talks/ruth_chang_how_to_make_hard_choices?language=en#t-6867)

- The PLUS Ethical Decision Making Model (https://www.ethics.org/resources/free-toolkit/decision-making-model)

- "Casual . . . Cool? Making Choices About Casual Sex" on Scarleteen (http://www.scarleteen.com/node/7244)

different kind of relationships. For example, within a teacher/student relationship, you're less likely to talk about your sexual or gender identity than you are within a sexual and romantic relationship. Nevertheless, if you want to build a strong relationship with someone, being honest with that person about yourself in ways that are relevant to your relationship is important.

When you're talking with a teacher, for example, it will hurt your relationship if you are dishonest about your long-term educational or professional interests. Your teacher won't be able to help you reach your goals if you aren't honest. Similarly, you will only hurt your sexual and romantic relationships if you aren't honest with yourself and your partner about what you're looking for in the context of that relationship. If you aren't honest with yourself about what you need, you won't be able to communicate with your partner. If you aren't honest with your partner about what you need, your partner won't be able to support you. Understanding who you are and what you need was a substantial piece of Chapter 7, but the need to honestly understand yourself goes beyond sexual decision making, and extends to all aspects of healthy relationships.

Knowing yourself and what you want allows you to move through life with confidence and clarity. Allowing your partner to know you requires trust in your partner. When they know the real you, your relationship can blossom with a new kind of support and source of joy and love.

Here's an example of a real-life realization about the need for honesty, and what it can potentially offer you:

A few years ago, I was talking with an extraordinary young woman who was very, very busy. She was an athlete at the highest level, and much of her time was spent training. Because of her training, she moved around often and struggled to build romantic relationships.

She finally found someone she connected with and was very devoted to him. She told me that he was very supportive of her career—he wasn't even upset when she had to train even more hours as a particularly important competition drew closer. I asked her what that meant to her, when he didn't get upset with her. She said that he just came over later than usual to have sex, after she got home from training, rather than get angry because he couldn't come over earlier.

I asked her what it looked like when her parents or her friends were being supportive of her career, and her answer was very different. She expected her parents and her friends to offer to do things for her, because she was too busy to get things done on her own. She expected them to understand that her attention would be elsewhere in the weeks leading up to a big event.

As this young woman was explaining what "supportive of her career" meant to her, she realized that she had very different expectations from her boyfriend than her friends. I offered her this vision of what a supportive boyfriend might look like in her life:

In the weeks leading up to an event, he might bring dinner to your training session and drop it off with a flower and a note saying he's impressed with your dedication. After a particularly hard day, he might come over to your house to give you a massage and tuck you into bed. He would text you encouraging notes, telling you he believes in you.

She almost gasped as I went through a few examples of what having a supportive partner could mean—and she agreed that kind of support sounded amazing. Unreal. Like a fairy tale in real life. A whole other kind of support than her boyfriend had given her so far. She decided on the spot to break up with him.

I suggested that instead of breaking up, she could ask him to do some of these things for her. If she didn't even know that she needed these things, how could he know? There are some people who have an intuitive sense of what someone else needs, but some people need to have it explained to them, and then they'd be happy to do it! The young

woman needed to be more honest with herself and then be more honest with her partner.

Before we get too pie-in-the-sky hopeful, though, let's bring some reality in. You won't always know what you want—that's to be expected. What you can hope for is that you will figure out what you need over time, and hopefully it will be accessible to you.

There will likely be times when you regret something that you've done or said or thought—and that might be because you didn't thoroughly consider your position or perspective, or it might be because you changed after learning something new. Sometimes people feel very badly about themselves when this happens. They feel like they could have or should have done something else or something more. I encourage you to work against these feelings of less-than. Instead, hold on to the idea that you did the best you could with the information and skills that you had. Dig in deep toward self-compassion. If you didn't do your best, strive to do your best going forward.

Talking

Share your thoughts with your partner. Share your thoughts with your parents and your friends and your mentors. Tell them who you are, in ways and places and times when it is safe to share yourself. Share what applies to the relationship that you are building together.

For some people, sharing personal things about themselves can feel inhibiting or be incredibly difficult. But it isn't impossible. The way to share who you are is something that you probably learned how to do as a toddler: Use your words. The first time honestly talking about who you are is usually the hardest, but for some people it never gets any easier. It does become more meaningful, though.

So, tell your partner about the things you want and the things you don't want, without feeling guilty. Tell them when you feel the most loved and what makes you laugh. Tell them what makes you sad and what hurts your feelings. Tell them what makes you want to touch them and what makes you want them to touch you.

SO, YOU MAY NOT KNOW THIS, BUT I'M A PERSON THAT DOESN'T LIKE TO TALK. I DON'T LIKE FEELINGS EITHER. I FEEL LIKE IT'S TOO MUCH WORK TO GET INTO THE GUSHY STUFF AND LEARN ABOUT IT, REMEMBER IT. IT'S A LOT IF WORK AND TIME INVESTED. SO I REALLY LIKE THIS GUY, AND THOSE DAMN FEELINGS ARE HAPPENING. CAUSE IT'S NOT JUST SEX I WANT FROM HIM, I WANT TO FEEL THE HEAT FROM HIS FINGERTIPS. I WANT TO KNOW IF HIS LIPS TASTE LIKE HONEY OR CHOCOLATE. THEN HE GIVES ME THIS LOOK, AND HE HOLDS IT THERE FOR LIKE 15 MIN, LIKE WHY??? I KNOW WHAT I WANT, I JUST DON'T KNOW HOW TO ASK FOR IT. I DON'T KNOW IF I SHOULD BE MY BLUNT SELF OR SUGARCOAT EVERYTHING LEADING UP TO THE DAY I ACTUALLY SAY SOMETHING. I DON'T KNOW, LIKE TODAY ONE OF MY ACQUAINTANCES, TOLD ME TODAY THAT SHE WANTS HER ~~XXXXXX~~ BOYFRIEND TO BE BETTER IN BED. SHE TELLS ME THAT HE DOESN'T USE ENOUGH LUBE AND SHE GETS HURT. I TOLD HER THAT SHE REALLY NEEDS TO SIT DOWN AND TALK TO HIM... LIKE LITERALLY BEAT IT INTO HIS MIND WITH YOUR EYES TYPE OF THING. I JUST HOPE THAT SHE DOESN'T GET HURT AGAIN. AS FOR MY COMMUNICATION SKILLS, I THINK I TELL HIM THAT WE SHOULD GET TO KNOW EACH OTHER AS A COUPLE... JEEZ I SOUND OLD.

MARGARET

And then ask them how they feel so you can learn about them; when they answer your questions, be sure to listen.

Talking Q's

1. Do you ever hesitate to tell someone about yourself? Why?

2. Have you ever told someone something new about yourself and had them think it was bad? Why did they think it was bad?

3. Have you ever not been sure about whether to tell someone about yourself, but then decided to tell them anyway? Did they think it was good? Why did it turn out to be a good thing?

4. How might you know whether telling someone something about yourself will be good or bad? (Pro tip: You can't always know, but you can try and guess by talking about that thing as an idea from a movie or a book or a friend and seeing how they react. It's not a guarantee on how they'll react when it's you, but it's not a bad start.)

Listening

Spend time really listening to what someone else has to say in response to what you say and in answer to your questions.

Listening is sometimes presented as simpler than it really is. There is more to listening than merely understanding the words at first glance. Listening on a deeper level, to the verbal and the nonverbal information, presented in the context of identity and relationship, is very involved. Listening means quieting your mind and listening to what the other person is saying with their words, their body, and their heart.

Listening is to shed your own thinking and come to a deeper understanding of another person's thinking. You will have time to consider your response to them once they have stopped talking. If you try to think of your answer before they have finished sharing, it is likely that you will miss something.

Listening Q's

1. Is there a particular person who you feel listens to you really, really well? What do they do that makes you feel heard?

2. Is there a particular person who you really like to listen and pay attention to when they are telling you something? What do you do when you are listening to that person compared to the ways that you listen to other people?

3. What are the benefits that you or someone else gains from being listened to really well?

4. What are the benefits that you or someone else gains from listening?

Coming Together
When you bring together these three things (being honest about yourself, talking, and listening) and when the person you are talking with is

able to do the same things for you, this is when beautiful, open, honest, supportive conversation happens. This is when the ebb and flow of dialogue and understanding come together to make beautiful music. This is communication in its highest form: an art form that brings people together.

Communication skills can take a lifetime to learn. It's important to keep working on them.

Additional Resources

There are so many resources on communication and how to do it better and more effectively! Whether or not a particular model of communication will resonate with you is likely based on your own instincts and preferences and what is a good match for you. Which is to say, if the resources here don't resonate with you, there are so many more available!

- "How to Speak So That People Want to Listen," a TED talk by Julian Treasure (https://www.ted.com/talks/julian_treasure_how_to_speak_so_that_people_want_to_listen)

- "Listening to Shame," a TED talk by Brené Brown (https://www.ted.com/talks/brene_brown_listening_to_shame)

I just got off the phone with my cousin T. It's been a while since we talked and as always we were catching up and she was talking about my ~love life~. I told her that I'm dating B and she was asking if we had had sex—so I gave her all the juicy details that she wanted to hear! Later, she told me that her husband never goes down on her or really cares about whether she orgasms or not. So I asked her if she had orgasms at all and she said "rarely".

And that is, so, so weird to me!!! I guess maybe I'm just a pretty outspoken person and know what I want and have never been in a relationship where there was "orgasm inequality". Even before B, I almost always had an orgasm. At that time, I had an ok self-image but it wasn't amazing—and in-between those periods of feeling great, I had long periods of self-doubt. It didn't help that my life at that time was insanely stressful with school, and that I had gained about 15 pounds over the course of the year from stress eating and not sleeping. Fast forward three years and I've lost all the weight (yay for walking everywhere

ANJALI

instead of driving). But that isn't the most important change.

The most important change was coming to ~~terms~~ with _me_. My body, my opinions, goals, thoughts, and feelings, and just realizing that this is ~~the~~ ME* and I need to get familiar with myself, because I'm awesome and sexy, and beautiful and damn if anyone has the fucking right to make me feel like shit. This realization came after so, so many episodes of a boyfriend or "friend" or family member telling me that I look puffy, or tired, or could "use some make up". I love my curves (hello, bootylicious butt), my strong legs from dancing, my voluptuous (I love that word!!) boobs, and everything in between. Yeah, my stomach is not totally ~~flat~~ flat but who the hell cares? I can dance for hours, I work out 5 times a week, I'm running my own photography business and working full time and I'm AWESOME :)

The point is, all this soul-searching happened right around the time that I started with B, and when we had sex for the first time, I was so, so ready. I felt incredibly sexy and ready to bare it all to B. We've been together for a couple of months now, and the sex is absolutely electrifying. I always feel sexy and amazing around him, and he's absolutely great too and always makes me feel sexy. We have such great chemistry, and from the very beginning we've been very open to each other about what we want and what we like while we're having sex. I have no problems asking him to go harder, to slow down, to move his hand so it hits my clit just so — whatever. Because honestly, when you're baring it all to someone else and getting intimate with them, why would you hold back? Pleasure is a two-way street and both partners absolutely deserve to get _exactly_ what they need, and communication is so, so important. It's not always easy, and things aren't always picture perfect — I love how much laughter B and I share when we're having sex because nothing is off-limits, and we get adventurous and try crazy positions and new things and it doesn't always go well — but we share a laugh and keep it moving. And it certainly doesn't hurt that I am insanely attracted to B and he has this way with his tongue and fingers and other body parts hehehehe. Now if you'll excuse me, I have a new, insanely gorgeous black lace bra from Victoria's Secret that a certain someone is dying to take off ;)

Chapter 9

Healthy Relationships 101

What do healthy and unhealthy relationships even look like? It's not something that is always obvious when looking at relationships portrayed in the media or even in real life. While relationships that are very healthy or very unhealthy are often obvious, those that are somewhere in between, or have aspects of both, are much more difficult to notice, particularly when you're in love. This chapter offers ways to figure out what's healthy and what's unhealthy, along with places to reach out to if you think you are in an unhealthy relationship.

 Note: Reading about healthy and unhealthy relationships can be emotional if you are close to an unhealthy one. If you are worried about your relationship, I hope that you will read over this chapter a little bit at a time. Don't overwhelm yourself, but do be honest with yourself. If you are worried about the health of a friend's or family member's relationship, remember that it can be painful to acknowledge being in an unhealthy relationship. There's more to follow on how to process and move forward if you or someone who you are close to is in an unhealthy relationship.

Much of what is included in this chapter is framed in the context of romantic and/or sexual relationships, but it applies to many other kinds of relationships, too. It is not merely intimate relationships that can be healthy and unhealthy—all relationships can be. Thinking about which relationships are best and most supportive for you is a process you will go through your entire life. Indeed, family relationships, friendships, and professional and academic relationships all have the potential to be healthy or unhealthy, or to have aspects of both. Considering the guidelines of what a healthy relationship looks like as they apply to the other kinds of relationships is a good place to start when evaluating any of your connections. There are different ways to think about healthy and unhealthy relationships. For example, The Duluth Model is a very well-known and respected model of healthy and unhealthy relationships (http://www.theduluthmodel.org/training/wheels.html). There are also organizations who write and talk about healthy relationships without a model (http://www.thehotline.org/is-this-abuse/healthy-relationships/). In fact, there are a thousand ways to talk about healthy and unhealthy relationships, and a million ways to be in healthy and unhealthy relationships. In this book, we will talk about columns and shadows.

Columns and Shadows

Sometimes people need different things from a relationship for it to be healthy. Whether to wait for marriage to have sex is an example of something that some people need and other people don't. However, the Columns and Shadows model says that a healthy relationship is always shaped by the following four behaviors and attitudes: respect, equality, safety, and trust. Each of these has the potential to be a column holding up a strong and healthy relationship or they can be a shadow that only pretends to be the real thing.

While these four categories (respect, equality, safety, and trust) are common enough words, I think it's still worthwhile to define them so we all know exactly what we're talking about.

- **Respect:** a deep admiration of someone because of their skills, abilities, and identity; treating someone the way they want/need/ deserve to be treated.

- **Equality:** having the same amount of power and agency in the relationship as the other person.

- **Safety:** a feeling and knowledge that your physical, emotional, and mental wellbeing are being attended to.

- **Trust:** confidence that another person is living with integrity regarding your relational agreements.

Each of these four columns can address a wide range of topics, like money, sexual decision making, friends, foods you eat together, and yes, whether you look at each other's cell phones.

Here are a few more examples:

Respect: One partner likes to dance, but the other partner doesn't.

- **Column:** "It's cool that you like dancing. It's not really my thing. Do you want to meet up after you're done?"

- **Shadow:** "It's weird that you like dancing; I don't like it at all. You should come hang out with me instead. I always want to spend my time with you. Don't you like spending time with me?"

Equality: One partner knows a lot about movies and the other one doesn't. They agreed that going to a movie one night would be fun.

- **Column:** "Since I know more about movies, let me tell you a little bit about the ones that are playing right now, and then we can decide together which one to see tonight."

- **Shadow:** "Since I know more about movies, I am going to decide which one we see tonight. If there were something you knew more about, you could make the decision about that."

Safety: One partner wants to have sex and the other one doesn't.

- **Column:** "Of course it's okay that you don't want to have sex to-night. How would you feel about holding each other?"

- **Shadow:** "What do you mean you don't feel like having sex tonight? I thought you loved me! I need to have sex, and so if you won't have sex with me, it means you don't want me to feel safe with you!"

Trust: One partner is always late and forgets to call. They promise not to be late to their partner's birthday party and then are late.

- **Column:** "I'm so sorry. There's nothing I can say to make this bet-ter, and I know that. I'm going to start setting alerts on my phone so I won't be late again. Happy birthday and I love you."

- **Shadow:** "Yeah, I know I said I wouldn't be late, but it's not like anyone noticed, did they? This wouldn't even matter if you didn't make such a big deal out of nothing. Don't you trust me?"

friends and family is a common experience in an unhealthy relationship. It's one of the things that happens when several of the categories
of shadows start to work together and it increases the unhealthiness
until it becomes abusiveness.

What Is Gaslighting?

Gaslighting is when someone, usually a romantic or sexual partner,
makes you question your own knowledge and memory, and it can be a
very unhealthy part of a relationship. The term comes from a play, *Gaslight,* which was later adapted into film. In *Gaslight,* a husband works
to convince his wife and everyone around them that she is insane by
changing her environment and telling her she is wrong when she no-
tices the changes. In one example, he dims the gaslights in their house.
When she comments on this, he tells her that she is seeing it wrong,
and the lights haven't been dimmed at all.

It can be difficult for someone experiencing a relationship shadow
like gaslighting to identify and label it as "unhealthy." At its very core,
gaslighting is designed to undermine a person's intuition, trust, and
belief in themselves. While some forms of gaslighting, like the one from
the play, might seem obvious from the outside, they aren't always easy
to see from the inside of a relationship. Here's an example of what another instance of gaslighting might look like:

*You're running late to meet up with your partner and some friends at a
restaurant. As you're walking up to the table, you see that your partner is
leaning in close to one of your friends and has their hand on your friend's
leg. After dinner, you ask your partner about it. "What? You're crazy. I wasn't
doing that. You're seeing things. Why don't you trust me?"*

This is a common example of gaslighting. Instead of addressing the
actual issue that was brought up, whether it is personal space, agreed-
on monogamy, or something else, the "gaslighter" makes the conversation all about the faults and perceptions of the "gaslightee." When
gaslighting occurs, it's also common for the gaslighter to assume the
part of the victim who isn't getting any trust. Another common fea-
ture of gaslighting may involve contradicting someone's report of their
emotions. Here's another example of gaslighting:

You and your older sibling are sorting through old movies at your house. You pick up a horror film and show it to your sibling. "Hey, you remember all of these scary movies you used to make me watch and how much I hated them?" you ask. Your sibling dismisses you, saying "No way. You loved those. You're just remembering it wrong, since you always like to make me into the bad guy."

There are multitudes of healthy ways to acknowledge and respect different perspectives and viewpoints while still disagreeing with someone. One of the easiest ways to do this is to explicitly tell someone "Your feelings are valid" and "I value your perspective." Going back to the initial scenario given on gaslighting, here's an example of how that could have worked out in a much more positive, healthy way:

You're running late to meet up with your partner and some friends at a restaurant. As you're walking up to the table, you see that your partner is leaning in close to one of your friends and has their hand on your friend's leg. After dinner, you ask your partner about it. They pause for a moment, then say, "I am so sorry. I was making a joke with your friend. Looking at it from your perspective, though, I can definitely see why it might worry you and why you would want to talk about it. If you want, we can go get some ice cream and talk about this more. Or we can not talk about it and just eat ice cream. It's your call!"

So, what to do if you recognize that someone you're in a relationship with is engaging in gaslighting behavior? Or, what if a friend or a loved one is in a relationship that features gaslighting? The National Domestic Violence Hotline and LoveisRespect.org (listed on page 168) both have information on gaslighting and are available for advice. You can also discuss this with a trusted individual in your personal life, like a friend, family member, or mental health professional.

What About Intent?

Another reason unhealthy behaviors like gaslighting might be hard to identify in a relationship is because it's possible the other person is not intentionally engaging in them. A gaslighting dynamic doesn't have to be intentionally created to be unhealthy. Someone who is engaging in gaslighting may not recognize that they're using manipulative behavior, or even know that their behavior is a form of manipulation. But just because there's a lack of intent doesn't mean there is a lack of harm.

yes pregnancy risk) or if hooking up means that all of the clothes stayed on and you kissed (no STI or pregnancy risk).

The term "hooking up" likely gained popularity exactly because of the lack of specificity around exactly what happens. If you're feeling awkward or shy describing your sexual activities, saying that you've hooked up can provide a safe way to indicate sexual intimacy without giving specifics. If you're less descriptive of what happened, you're less likely to be criticized for being either too sexual or not sexual enough. It stops some of the harsher cultural judgments around sexual activity (for more on this, read the note on "being a slut" and "being frigid" at the end of this section).

In some ways, hooking up has also taken some of the pressure off of the words "sex" and "virgin." Those words can feel too specific, while "hooking up" maintains the legitimacy of sexual desire without oversharing. In this way, hooking up fills a much needed language gap, although one that makes many adults very nervous, and can serve a very useful purpose. However, talking about hooking up can let people ignore or minimize the potential physical and emotional effects of sexual intimacy. That's a huge problem because the language becomes hurtful rather than useful.

One more point about the meaning of the phrase hooking up: It is usually understood within friend groups. That means your friends might all use the word to describe a certain set of sexual activities while another group of friends might use it to describe a different set of sexual activities. As long as everyone understands what it means, there's no problem with what language is used. But, it might be useful to double check that everyone does, in fact, understand the words hooking up the same way before you continue saying it.

Hookup Language

1. Have any of your friends ever hooked up with someone? If so, did you understand exactly what sexual acts they took part in when they said they hooked up?

2. Have you ever told your friends that you hooked up with someone? If so, are you sure that they knew what sexual acts you took part in?

3. Does it matter whether you or your friends know exactly which sexual acts you've taken part in when you say you've hooked up? Why or why not?

4. What are the pros and cons of using the words hooking up to describe a sexual experience? How can you use the language of hooking up and reduce the cons and benefit from the pros?

Here's where language around hooking up gets really tricky: When thinking about whether you actually want to hook up with someone, it's important not to assume that all hookups can or should include sex AND it's important not to assume that a hookup is only kissing. If someone suggests a hookup, you'll need to clarify their language BEFORE you hook up. Don't ask yourself whether you want to hook up with them. Ask yourself whether you want to kiss them or have them touch your breasts or take their pants off. Be specific. If you aren't specific and honest in your own thinking about what you want, you won't be able to be specific with the other person. Similarly, if you're actually having a conversation with the other person about whether you are going to hook up with them (and I hope you will have those conversations rather than just hooking up!), don't let the language be vague. This is all tied very closely to the idea of consent, which we will go into more detail about in Chapter 14.

The Act of Hooking Up

First, because it's clearly unclear, here is the definition of hooking up we will use for this chapter and this book:

Hooking up: Engaging in consensual sexual acts with another person. It usually refers to people who are not in a committed romantic relationship . . . May involve kissing, penetrative sex, or any other kind of sexual contact.

This description covers a lot of different kinds of sexual acts, of course! It can include everything from sexual touching over the clothes to penetrative sex. There's lots of details on the specifics of sexual activities in Section Three: Sex and Sex. If you want to jump ahead, that's a fine place to go. Just be sure to come back here eventually!

Sometimes it's important to be more specific about sexual activities, especially when talking about decision making, communication, and potential emotional and physical risks. In those cases, we will be more specific.

Hooking up is neither good nor bad. No one other than you can tell you whether hooking up is good or bad for you. That includes your friends, your family, the people who want to hook up with you, and the people you want to hook up with. While you might be interested in listening to what they have to say, you are not beholden to or obligated to follow their advice. Your decisions should take into account a number of questions:

- Who are you thinking about hooking up with?
- What are the risks involved in hooking up?
- What are your motivations for hooking up?
- How do you feel about hooking up/what are your values about hooking up?

Answering these questions might be easy or hard. You might find that you have easy answers to them one day and the next you're not sure any more or you have completely different answers. That evolution is natural, but you need to be sure that you're continuing to think about your answers rather than just going with the flow.

How Do You Feel About Hooking Up?

Some people are able to take the physical risks associated with hooking up in stride. They are educated about and confident in their STI and pregnancy prevention methods. They are comfortable with opening a conversation about recent sexual activities, STI testing, and STI and pregnancy prevention methods with hookup partners. They are confident about the kinds of sexual pleasure that they want to receive from hookups and feel that the benefits that hooking up brings to their lives are worth the physical risks. Other people feel exactly the opposite. They are hesitant to raise the subject of physical risk with a potential hookup partner, feel uneducated or untrusting of the risk reduction methods, and don't really know what they want or whether hooking up would be worth it. Some people might feel one way some of the time, with some hookup partners, and in some situations, while they feel the exact opposite other times. It is so important that you're able to listen to that piece of yourself that tells you whether you're confident and comfortable or not. If the risks might not be worth the experience, then it's not the right experience for you, and you have the right to say no. Actually, you have an obligation to yourself to say no.

For some people, hooking up feels right and healthy. Other people don't feel good hooking up. Here are three truths that are necessary for you to understand yourself, to be honest with yourself and to make effective decisions about hookups.

- Be as sexy or unsexy as feels right to you.

- Be as sexual or asexual as feels right to you.

- You know you best. Sometimes it's useful to talk with other people who know you well.

The most important thing is not whether you say yes or no or maybe or check back tomorrow to a hookup, but that you listen to and are respectful of your own internal compass of what's the right path for you and for your potential hookup partner. Everything from Chapter 9 on Healthy Relationships 101 applies to hookups too. They might be short relationships, but they are still relationships!

What Are the Risks Involved in Hooking Up?

There are four kinds of risk that you need to consider in all sexual acts, including hooking up: physical, emotional, social, and regret.

The physical risks of hooking up will depend on the specifics of the sexual acts that you engage in, of course, but it is an increased risk level over doing similar sexual activities with a monogamous partner. With a one-time hookup partner, you won't be as familiar with their sexual history as you could be with a long-term partner, and both of you are more likely to have a higher number of recent sexual experiences than if you were in a long-term, monogamous relationship. That said, physical risks can be reduced. Talking with a hookup partner—even briefly, and depending on what kinds of sexual activities you might engage in—about their recent sexual history, the last time they had an STI test, and condom use habits when they are relevant, is critical when there is a potential for fluid exchange in the sexual activities.

The emotional risks that come with hooking up have to do with whether you're acting in alignment with your values and the degree of closeness that you have or don't have with your hookup partner. If you aren't acting in alignment with your values—especially if you hook up when hooking up isn't something that you value as a healthy action for you—it can hurt you on an emotional and spiritual level. Don't assume that because it's not a physical risk, it matters less. It may, sometimes, matter even more. Doing right by yourself, within your value system, is important. It's also important to realize that your value system will probably evolve over time. If you have done something in the past that doesn't fit within your current value system, it can be hard to forgive yourself.

And then, there is social risk. Sexuality should be about you and who you are sexual with, not about the potential for rumors or how someone else might judge you. But, it's impossible to ignore the social factors in real life; you have very little influence over social risk. It is so common for someone to kiss another person—or even just to spend a few hours alone with them without any sexual contact—and then to see rumors spiral out of control about all kinds of sexual activities. So, you can't control the social risk, but you can be aware of it. Think about it when you're considering the risks of hooking up.

The final risk is that you might regret the hookup. It's a possibility. Not a pleasant one, of course, but not one that you can ignore. Asking yourself how you might feel the day after the hookup is an important step in considering whether you might feel regret. If you feel hesitation, or you think you might regret the decision to hookup the day after, it's worth saying no to the experience. There will be other opportunities! Ones that you'll be much more certain about and that you are less likely to regret.

If you do feel regret after some kind of sexual contact, whether it's a hookup or something with a long-term partner, be compassionate with yourself. Consider it a learning experience. Move forward with more information about yourself and know that you can make better decisions with your new self-knowledge.

Who Are You Thinking About Hooking Up With?

If you've decided that you want to have a hookup, the next thing to consider is who you are going to hook up with. Or you might have found a person who you want to hook up with, so the *who with* was answered before the *whether to.* But, just because someone is cute and flirts, doesn't mean that they're going to be a good person to hook up with—who they are and how they treat you matters just as much as sexual chemistry and attraction. In fact, the people in any kind of sexual or romantic relationship, whether it's a marriage or a hookup, are the most important thing. Is the relationship based in an abundance of respect, equality, safety, and trust? All aspects of a healthy relationship can and should apply to a hookup—to both you and the other person.

What these four components look like in a hookup is different from what they look like in a long-term relationship, of course. But, nevertheless, they are critical to both kinds of relationships.

Sometimes people hook up with someone after they've just met, and sometimes they hook up with someone they've known for a longer time but haven't been romantic or sexual with before. The kind(s) of sexual activities in any hookup may depend on how well you know the person. Maybe you'll hook up (kiss) someone you met recently, but hook up (have oral sex) with someone who you've been close friends with for a few years. The person and your personal knowledge of and experience with them will influence your decision on what kind of hookup you want to have.

Regardless of anything else, the person and how they talk with you, treat you, and touch you matters. You have the right to a healthy hookup, if that is what is right for you. You have the right to start hooking up with someone and to change your mind for any reason, including because they do not treat you the way that you want to be treated, not feeling *right,* or not having the physical chemistry that you had hoped for. Your hookup partner has the right to decide to end the hookup at any time and for any reason too. Being comfortable with and excited about all of the different kinds of physical and emotional intimacy that you engage in is the way that things should be! Anyone who doesn't respect that isn't ready to be in a relationship, whether it be long- or short-term.

A hookup, in all of its varied potential physical activities, has the potential to be healthy and the potential to be unhealthy. Think of it and consider whether it's meeting your needs for a healthy relationship in the same way that you might think about a long-term thing. Be choosy. Know what you want and talk with any potential hook-up partner, even if it's a short conversation, about what you both want from your hookup.

What Are Your Motivations for Hooking Up?

This question is ultimately the most important thing for you to think about as you're considering whether you want to hook up with someone *and* what kind of hookup you might be interested in. Are you feeling motivated because the hookup sounds really good to you or because someone is pressuring you into it? Sometimes the person who wants to hook up with you is the one to pressure you, but sometimes your friends are the ones. Sometimes people even pressure themselves into hooking up, because they feel like they haven't had the "right" level of experience yet. Whoever is pressuring, sexual pressure isn't good for you. In the best of all possible worlds, and you should hope for your sexual experiences to be the best of all possible worlds, you'll feel excited and happy about each of your sexual connections. If your motivation for a hookup has to do with someone else or something else other than the physical and emotional connection, then it's not right yet. There will, of course, be the right times and places for sexual connections if that is what you want—there's just no reason to rush yourself!

Pulling all of these ideas together, here are a few questions that you need to answer when you are thinking about a hookup:

Hookup Q's

1. Do you and your potential hookup partner agree on what kind of sexual contact you'd like to engage in?

2. Does hooking up in this way and at this time feel good to your internal moral and ethical compass?

3. What kind(s) of sexual activities do you want to include in the hookup?

4. What are the risk(s) associated with those sexual activities? What can you do to reduce those risks?

5. Who are you thinking about hooking up with?

6. Why are you thinking about hooking up?

in our cultural consciousness as it is unlikely to happen. While lots of people think that outmoded dating outline is how things should go, here's what's actually happening for most people:

- Two teenagers hang out at school/a friend's house/church/work/online/etc.

- Teenagers enjoy each other's company and spend more time in person and/or online together.

The clarity and definition of dating is missing, for sure. But, this is the path that modern relationships among people of all ages are taking and it's not necessarily a bad thing.

When cultural expectations lack clarity in roles, relationships, and expectations, as ours does, there is value to the more fluid approach that is currently popular. It allows people to try out relationships without as much social or personal risk. It provides more ways for people who are questioning their own identities—be they gender or sexual identities—to take part more easily. It reduces the stigma for people who aren't interested or aren't making romantic or sexual connections. In addition to these welcoming perspectives, in the current model, couples that want more clarity can still achieve it.

If you're interested in starting something with someone, here are a few frequently asked questions.

Who's Supposed to Ask Who Out?

Because the cultural concept of a date is old fashioned, it's hard to say who's supposed to ask who out. We could fall back on the old-fashioned rules, which say that the boy is supposed to ask the girl out, end of conversation. But that doesn't make a lot of sense if you like a boy and you want to ask him out. And, it doesn't make any sense if you're interested in women and/or if you're trans and not out and/or if you're gender non-binary and/or many, many other problems with the boy-asks-girl rule. A strict understanding of gender roles just doesn't hold water anymore, which adds to the confusion around the entire dating paradigm in the first place. If you can't figure out who's supposed to ask who out, of course dating as a cultural practice is going to fall away.

So, here's the answer: A person who likes another person is supposed to be the one to reach out. Not necessarily to ask the other person on a date, but to express interest, to gauge the other person's interest, and to suggest that they spend some time together.

How Do You Ask Someone?

You ask someone by being emotionally vulnerable, clearly communicating your interest, and being honest about your interest in them. You use the communication skills you have at hand to invite the person you're interested in to be emotionally vulnerable, to clearly communicate their interest, or lack thereof, in you, and to be honest with you.

Another way to think about this process is that you are inviting someone into a space of exploring a healthy relationship, whether that intended relationship be a short hookup, a longer relationship, or an exploration of the options. Here are some details on how to go about that invitation:

Express Your Emotions

Emotions are tricky. When asking someone out, you need to tell them about your feelings without knowing their feelings, or at least without being sure of their feelings. The potential for rejection exists when you ask someone to hang out with you. If you don't know a person very well, you may worry that rejection will be harsh or dismissive. In those situations, it can be easier to not express why or how much you want to spend time with that person. You might decide to ask for something lower-stakes, like inviting them to a party that you're throwing or to participate in some other large group activity with you and your friends. These kinds of activities are never a bad idea for the first time hanging out with someone.

Communicate Clearly

If you were to walk up to your person of interest and start talking, but interrupt yourself several times to start again, to apologize for taking

OH, SEVENTH GRADE. HOW I DON'T MISS YOU. MOST OF MY MEMORIES FROM THAT TIME MAKE ME FEEL UNCOMFORTABLY EMBARRASSED. THE MOST EMBARRASSING MEMORY FROM THAT TIME IS THE CRUSH I HAD ON A GUY WHO WAS IN ALL OF MY CLASSES. HE HAD HARDLY ANY PERSONALITY. IT'S KIND OF AS IF MY BRAIN WENT, "ALRIGHT, WE'RE IN A NEW SCHOOL! THAT MEANS WE NEED TO PICK A NEW PERSON TO CRUSH ON. LET'S DO IT THE EASY WAY: EENIE MEENIE MINEY MO, I CHOOSE YOU!"

MY FRIENDS KNEW ABOUT THE CRUSH OF COURSE, & WHEN THE VALENTINE'S DAY DANCE CAME UP THEY ENCOURAGED ME TO ASK HIM TO BE MY DATE. EVEN THE THOUGHT OF IT MADE ME EMBARRASSED & ASHAMED. HOW DARE I, A WEIRD OBESE GIRL, ASK OUT A THIN, CONVENTIONALLY ATTRACTIVE MALE! HE'D REJECT ME RUDELY & LAUGH ABOUT IT TO ALL OF HIS FRIENDS, I WAS ABSOLUTELY SURE. & I'M STILL PRETTY SURE HE WOULD HAVE; HE WAS (& STILL IS) A GIANT JERK.

THE BODY POSITIVE MOVEMENT HAS TAUGHT ME SO MANY THINGS, & I'M THINKING MORE ABOUT THOSE FEELINGS. SOMETIMES I'M STILL AMAZED AT HOW TREMENDOUSLY GROWING UP FAT REALLY AFFECTED ME, ESPECIALLY IN REGARDS TO MY RELATIONSHIPS WITH OTHERS. EVEN NOW, I KNOW IF I EVER WANTED TO BE IN A ROMANTIC/SEXUAL RELATIONSHIP WITH SOMEONE I WOULD PROBABLY CHICKEN OUT & THINK THAT I WAS TOO UGLY & FAT TO DESERVE THAT PERSON'S ATTRACTION. I'M ACTIVELY WORKING ON SEEING MYSELF AS MORE THAN A BAG OF ADIPOSE CELLS. IT CAN TAKE A LIFETIME TO UNLEARN DANGEROUS THOUGHT PROCESSES.

JORDAN

their time, and then to say never mind and walk off, you've missed an opportunity to communicate with clarity. To avoid this sort of thing, plan out what you're going to say before you start talking or texting.

Be Honest

If you know that you are ready to start something with someone, you should let them know that. If you want to get to know someone better with the hope of eventually having something more serious, be clear about that intention. You could tell them that you think they're cool and you want to get to know them better. Regardless of what your interest is, it's so important to be honest about it.

What. About. Prom??

It seems that every invitation to prom is bigger—although maybe not better—than the one before it. From group song and dance numbers, to costumes, to dozens and dozens of roses, asking someone to prom has become a huge event. These traditions can be fun to do and fun to remember, or they can be stressful to do, and if the answer is no, the memory can be painful.

When you are preparing a prom invitation (promposal!!), balance your personality with your potential date's personality. You'll need to do something that you enjoy and feel comfortable doing and that your potential date will enjoy and feel comfortable with. This is particularly true if the proposal is very public. Embarrassing your date in the asking process probably won't get you the answer that you hope for.

If you do decide to go big, you might want to do some preliminary work hinting or asking around about your potential date's inclination to say yes. Nothing is worse than a big public invitation when the answer is no.

Going big is not necessarily a bad thing! For the right person, with the right trimmings that are designed specifically with your date in mind, it can be very beautiful and meaningful. Be romantic! It's what promposals are for!

What If You're the One Who's Being Asked?

First things first: Do you want to say yes or no, or are you not sure what you want to say? Regardless of what your answer is, you should express your emotions, communicate clearly, and be honest.

Yes?

Don't hesitate to be honest about your excitement. If you're worried about coming off as too excited, you can scale back a little bit, but don't make it seem like you don't care either way. Do let the person asking you know that you're happy they asked and that you're looking forward to spending time with them. There's no reason for the person to think that you don't care about spending time with them or not—they've already put themselves in a place of vulnerability by reaching out to you. Responding with as much excitement as they showed when they asked you out is a good thing.

No?

You should be clear when you're saying no. Saying no isn't nearly as fun as saying yes. With a yes, you can both be excited. With a no, at least one of you is going to be disappointed, and it's hard to be the one who disappoints, especially if you know and are fond of the other person. Nevertheless, it is kinder to say no sooner rather than to allow someone to think that you're interested when you're not.

If you're saying no, be clear rather than deflecting. This means that you can't say that you're busy—they'll assume they should ask you to hang out another time. You shouldn't tell them that you've already seen that movie or that you don't like mini golf or that particular band—they'll try to find an activity that you do like. So you have to tell them:

- I don't want to take our relationship to that place.
- I appreciate your interest, but I don't return it. I hope you find someone who does.
- Whatever other feelings you have, as long as you express them kindly and clearly.

You can and should say no to someone without being mean or cruel. You may find additional support for this process in Chapter 13 on ending relationships.

Not Sure?

Maybe you're been taken by surprise when someone shows interest in spending more time with you, either because they're not someone who you know well or you just weren't expecting that they felt that way about you. Maybe you'll have an answer that bubbles to the surface, in which case you should give that answer, but maybe you won't even know what to say. If you're not sure what to say, then you'll need to say that. Your answer can be: "Um, I'm not sure. I'll need to get back to you." There's nothing wrong with saying that you need to think about it. If the person pressures you for an immediate answer, then the answer becomes clear: No. Because pressure beyond your comfort level isn't cool.

New Relationship Energy

It's important, when you're just starting something with a new person, that you know about New Relationship Energy (NRE). This refers to that nervous, excited feeling that you have when you're first getting to know someone new in a romantic or sexual way. That first blush of excitement can make you want to put all of your time, attention, and energy into that new person rather than a more balanced integration into your existing activities and friendships.

NRE can be really fun and engaging. It can breathe life into you, make you feel tingly, and invite you to see and understand your world in new ways.

NRE can be a problem because you might think that the relationship is falling apart when the NRE fades—even though that's a natural process. NRE may seduce you to engage in sexual activities that you might otherwise not do because of the fun and excitement and newness.

So while you don't need to try and stop yourself from feeling NRE, it is important to remember that's what's happening and not let yourself run away with it. Remember to pay attention to your other thinking about being in a long-term romantic and/or sexual relationship with a specific person. Whether your relationship is primarily romantic, sexual, or a combination of both will impact the degree to which the following points about public and private aspects of relationships are true for you. As you are reading through the next two mini-sections, think about which parts are most present and important to your relationship.

Relationships Go Public

Relationships are public in that your friends, family, and other important people in your life should be aware of your partner. This doesn't happen immediately, of course, but over time, being in a relationship has social implications because that's the way our culture and society are built. Your special someone will have public responsibilities to you, and you will have public responsibilities to them. This doesn't mean that as soon as you start dating, you'll be required to attend Christmas dinner, but after enough time, that is what many people want. At the start of a relationship, there are usually smaller public commitments like meeting friends, being supportive of personal interests, and talking with each other about work, school, family, and friends. Sometimes this means something simple, like listening to your partner when they've had a bad day. Sometimes it's more about things like trying not to be late, which could leave your partner embarrassed and waiting for you. Eventually there may be more, like going to church, attending a play that they are part of, or having dinner with your partner's family.

What kinds of people you and your partner are will decide which of these, or other potential public responsibilities, are most important to your specific relationship. You will need to consider both what you want from each other and what you're willing or able to do for each other. Here are a few questions to get the two of you started. If you are in a relationship, consider your answers to these questions as if you weren't in a relationship so that you can think about what you need as an individual.

Public Relationship Q's

1. What are ways that you engage in public that are important to you? (Example: performances, parties, family, church, school events, etc.)

2. Which of those ways of public engagement are important for you to have a partner to join you in?

3. How might you be willing to support your partner in their public engagements?

4. Are there public ways or places where you would not be willing to support your partner?

When a certain kind of public relationship is really important to one person, and their partner isn't willing or able to be part of that public role, the relationship isn't a good match. For example, if it is important to one person that they attend church with their partner, but the other person is an atheist and feels uncomfortable in church, that's not a good match. Another problematic match is someone who is highly social and wants to spend most nights with friends and wants their partner to be part of that experience, but their partner is uncomfortable in large groups of people and would rather hang out with one person or stay home. None of the four people in those two examples is wrong—they just need to find someone who is a better match for their public relationship needs.

conversation about a problem makes it worse. So, talk with a friend or two, write in your journal, figure out what you want and need to say, and start a conversation rather than delaying it.

One of my favorite quotes is from Mae West who said, "I never said it would be easy, I only said it would be worth it." While I don't think she was talking about relationships and communication, it's true here and in so many other places in life.

What if the problem isn't one that you can come to an agreement on or negotiate a middle ground? It might mean that it's time for the relationship to end. While that might be sad, it doesn't have to be devastating. You can have a successful relationship that ends kindly, compassionately, and clearly when it's no longer serving you and/or your partner. See Chapter 13, Ending Relationships, for more details, including what to do if you or the other person cheated.

Can Teenagers Fall in Love?

When adults say that teenagers can't fall in love, I want to banish them from working or talking with teens until they learn how to listen to teenagers. What an insulting statement! To say that someone "doesn't really know what love is" because they're too young is one of the worse forms of ageism[1].

Of course teenagers can fall in love and be in love. Anyone who tells you otherwise is being absurd.

There are differences between a fifteen-year-old in love with someone they've been dating for six months and a sixty-year-old in love with the person they've been married to for thirty years. Everyone agrees about that. But, there are also differences between a sixty-year-old in love with someone they've been dating for six months rather than someone they've been married to for thirty years. The difference has less to do with age and more to do with the length of the relationship.

---

[1]You can read more about discrimination against young people here: https://www.freechild.org/discrimination-against-youth-voice/

Listen to your heart. If you feel in love, then you are in love.

The regrettable thing is that being in love with someone does not always mean that it is a good or a healthy relationship. You can be in love with someone you are in an unhealthy relationship with. And I hope that you'll listen when you know that a relationship isn't good or right, even when you are deeply in love.

Finding "the One"

Everyone knows the high school sweetheart story. It's so romantic! To meet and be each other's first loves, and then to stay together—or to part ways only to get back together years or decades later! But it's not common and usually it wouldn't even be a good thing. The point of dating in high school, and sometimes in middle school and college, is less about finding that one, long-term relationship to stand the test of time and more about being social, enjoying your time with peers, and figuring yourself out. If you haven't tried being in a relationship yet it can be hard to know what you want, what is nice, what is a deal-breaker, what you have to give, and what you want to give. The likelihood of stumbling into a perfect match that will last for many decades is statistically unlikely. Not to say it never happens—because it does—but rather, that you shouldn't count on it, or even hope for it, to happen to you. Because, much like playing the lottery, living in hope of finding the one-and-only can diminish your enjoyment of life in the moment and an awareness of when it's time to move on.

Finding Balance

Sometimes relationships can be all-out romantic in ways that make your knees melt or make you want to reach even more romantic heights so that your partner's knees will melt even further. Sometimes this is good and sometimes this is problematic. Which one it is has to do with whether the romance is feeding both partners' needs in healthy ways and whether it is sustainable in the long run.

Because people need different things in relationships, the balance they find must take everyone's needs into account. For example, some people really love to be romantic toward their partner and other people and jump to that section. I will be addressing you, the reader, as if you are thinking about breaking up with someone or have recently been broken up with. If you're not in either of those situations, just pretend like I'm talking to future you, or a future friend who needs your support.

Should You End It?

How do you know when a relationship has run its course? It's a painful and important question to consider. Here are a few questions to start off with.

Should You End It Q's

1. When the relationship started, how did you feel about the other person?

2. How do you feel about the person now?

3. Are you thinking about ending the relationship because you feel that it's entirely over or because there is a problem that you don't want to or don't know how to address?

4. Imagine yourself a year from now, still in this relationship. How do you feel?

5. Imagine yourself a year from now, not having been in this relationship for a year. How do you feel?

6. What do the people who know and love you think about you ending this relationship?

Questions 1 and 2 go together. All relationships that last for very long will involve an evolution of feelings about the other person and about the relationship itself. Ideally, everyone's feelings will involve increased respect, deeper understanding, and more emotional openness. If the way that you felt in the beginning of the relationship, compared to how you feel now, shows a progression toward closeness rather than a negative progression, that's a good indication of a positive relationship. Long-term relationships often include a change in the urgency of spending large amounts of time with each other, or of having lots of sexual contact. That change isn't the same as not caring about the other person; it's actually an indication of your attachment deepening. When those desires and urgencies drop below a certain level (and what that level is varies a lot from person to person), then it suggests a problem. So think about whether you've found a healthy balance that isn't in the heat of the New Relationship Energy, but also hasn't dropped so low that all of the sparkly connection has drained out of the relationship.

Regarding Question 3: Sometimes people end relationships because they don't know how to fix a problem that really needs to be fixed—but if it's not fixed in this relationship, it's just going to pop up again in your next relationship. Some examples of this include not wanting to talk to or see your partner regularly, preferring your friends over your partner at all times, preferring your partner over your friends at all times, being jealous of your partner's friends, and so on. If you are building your relationships with shadows rather than columns, there's a problem in your approach rather than a problem with one specific relationship. Ending the relationship rather than dealing with the issues might not help in the long run, because sometimes you need to work through problems. However, sometimes you need to end the relationship first, in order to work through the problems, because they're mostly about you.

Questions 4 and 5 also go together and speak to your long-term goals, hopes, and dreams. Do you feel like your partner supports all those? Will you be happier and more fulfilled if you are together, or will you not be living to your fullest potential?

Question 6 helps you pull wisdom and insight from your community. While it is not always the best source of information, if you are lacking clarity, your community can sometimes provide support. Talking with connection. It's easy to have longer-term expectations of the relationship than there ends up being. Maybe you were looking forward to the parties, trips, school plays, or inside jokes. Maybe you were looking forward to the touch and the sex. Maybe you were looking forward to things even further away like marriage or babies. Maybe you were looking forward to emotional or physical connections that never even happened, but you thought they would. If you have hoped for these things, realizing that the relationship is over is realizing that those hopes are gone. It can be painful, moving away from what you hoped or even expected would happen.

If this is what you're feeling, this loss of hopes and dreams, it can be hard to acknowledge that the ending needs to happen.

They're Ending It

One of the quotes that you'll hear said when people are trying to comfort someone or in memes strewn across the internet or when you're watching *The Sound of Music* is:

"When God closes a door, he always opens a window."

It means that when a relationship ends, there's always a new beginning on its way. But it's not usually a comforting thing to hear. It means that you've had a door closed, and you're still standing there, looking at that now closed-off space.

If the belief that there is another path for you feels good and meaningful, if you feel that it points toward a hopeful future, listen to it. Find those cheerful, supportive memes and relish them.

If the sentiment drives you batty, that's okay. You may not want that new beginning. You may not want this time to consider yourself or what you want. You may want exactly what you had. Or rather, what you thought you had. It's okay to be angry. It's okay to be hurt.

Letting yourself feel angry, hurt, and whatever other emotions you may find bubbling up will allow you to find peace and to feel okay again at some point. Even when a relationship ending feels desperate, feeling okay again happens at some point. But, you can't rush it or make it happen.

How Long Does It Take to Feel Okay Again?

It depends on a lot of things. There's a rumor going around that it takes about a month per year that you were together before you feel better. Which means that if you dated someone for a month, it should only take you 1/12th of a month, or about two days, to get over them. Or if you dated someone for six months, it should take about two weeks. I think this is a pretty insulting way of talking about how long it takes before someone is ready to move on or is happy alone.

For example, if you dated someone for six months, but the last two months of that you were trying to figure out how to break up with them, it probably won't take you two weeks to feel okay again. But, if you dated someone for six beautiful, enthralling months—someone you'd been in love with for years—and then they suddenly broke up with you and started dating your BFF, all the while trying to be friends with and supportive of you, it might take you much longer than two weeks to move on.

The real answer is that you should feel free to take some time and mourn the end of the relationship. Feel all of your feelings. Talk with your friends and other confidants about your feelings. Write and draw about them. And then get yourself back up and start engaging in activities again. Do the things you love. Talk, write, and make art about new and different things. Even if it doesn't feel natural to move on, it helps to go through the motions. Your emotions will follow along eventually[1].

---

[1]There are lots of ways that people go about healing. Here's one example of how someone pulled herself up and out of depression: https://www.ted.com/talks/hannah_brencher_love_letters_to_strangers

Things Just . . . Ending

Sometimes no one ends a relationship, the people just drift apart. One day you look up and realize that you aren't as close to someone as you used to be. This is more common with friendships than it is with romantic or sexual relationships, but it also happens in those situations. This is usually far less of a fiery ending than when one person deliberately puts a stop to a relationship, but it doesn't mean that it's less painful in the end. There are still hopes and dreams that aren't realized. There are still inside jokes that no one will laugh with you about again. There are still ways and times to be sad and angry and everything else. With no one to blame, with no resolution, what happens next? Sometimes you don't get a resolution, you just get an ending.

Making Your Own Ending

If you feel like you don't really know why or how a relationship ended, or the other person didn't talk with you about it, or the things they said didn't make sense, sometimes you have to create your own ending. You can do this by talking it out with a friend or a counselor or someone else. If you find yourself really struggling to look forward rather than back at a failed relationship, there are other ways to move on. Here's one example of what it might look like:

Gather up the paper things that came from that person or distinctly remind you of that person—photographs and notes, for example. If they're online, print them out and then delete the digital files. If you don't have memories of this kind, write descriptions of some of the times you spent together on paper. Find a safe place to have a fire (a fireplace or designated campfire pit are best, with water on hand in case you need it), and lay the papers between the firewood. Before you light the fire, gather up all of the other things you may have that came from that person or distinctly remind you of that person. Throw them

away somewhere that you can't get them back again, like in a public dumpster. Return to your prepared fire. Say good-bye. Say all of the things that you wish you had been able to say. Light the fire. When the memories are gone, pick yourself up and make a new memory. Maybe that means going out with friends or maybe it means planting a garden. Whatever it is, do it for yourself as something you will look back on with joy rather than sadness.

Someone Cheated . . . Now What?

Many people think that if someone cheats during a romantic or sexual relationship, the relationship must end. But, does someone cheating always mean that you should break up with them/they should break up with you? Well, no, not always. Let's clarify a point about cheating: At its most basic, it means that someone's trust has been broken. Healing from that is a process, and it can't always be done. Here are the questions you should begin with before knowing whether to end the relationship.

Cheating Q's

1. How committed are you to the relationship? How committed is the other person?

2. Did both people have a clear understanding that the "cheating activity," whatever it was, would be considered cheating?

3. Did the cheating put either of you at physical risk for STIs, pregnancy, or other sexual health issues?

4. Was the cheating done in a way to embarrass or hurt you socially?

5. Is forgiveness a possibility?

Your answer to Question 1 will give guidance for whether you even need to continue answering the other questions. If this isn't a relationship that is important to you or the other person, and you feel like your trust has been broken or you have broken their trust, it's probably time to move on. If, however, both of you are committed to trying to work the relationship out, that's an opening for continued dialogue.

Question 2 gets to the crux of the cheating issue that many couples run into without realizing it. Here's an example of how this can play out: One person might consider it cheating if their partner dances intimately with someone else, while the other person considers it a friendly, non-cheating activity. The answer to this question is clear if the cheating activity was oral sex or another intimate sexual activity; those activities are more generally understood to be cheating. But short of kissing, if you consider something to be cheating, you need to have an explicit conversation about that with your partner.

If the cheating activities put either of your sexual health or emotional social stability at risk, that's a clear and substantial problem that doubles up on the emotional trust that was broken. To rebuild trust around sexual health is a process that can't be ignored. If this has happened, it will take time and communication to move past the hurt and the lack of trust.

If forgiveness is not possible, then it's definitely time to move on. This doesn't need to be a long, drawn out process. You can acknowledge that this particular relationship can't be healed and both people will be better off on their own.

But, what if both of you have cheated? Well, then both of you will have some things to process about your own choices and about your capacity to trust the other. Maybe you will both be able to let go of the hurt more easily because you understand. Maybe you are both uninterested in each other and it's time for a mutually agreed upon ending. Maybe your relationship shouldn't be monogamous. Maybe you should break up. Maybe you should work on your agreement to be monogamous. There are lots of possibilities. The only way to know for sure is to talk together, to think on your own, and to discover where your future might lead.

A General Note on the Concept of Monogamy

It's not always the right choice for everyone. For some people, being monogamous is something that doesn't fit with the ways that they interact with people. If you are one of those people who feels like you fall in love many times and with many people at the same time, you might be someone who is non-monogamous by nature. This isn't a bad thing. But it is something to learn more about and to be honest about, with yourself and with your partners[2].

Additional Resources

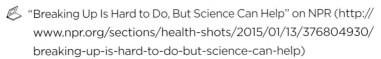 "Breaking Up Is Hard to Do, But Science Can Help" on NPR (http://www.npr.org/sections/health-shots/2015/01/13/376804930/breaking-up-is-hard-to-do-but-science-can-help)

 "Breakups Aren't All Bad: Coping Strategies to Promote Positive Outcomes" from the American Psychological Association (http://www.apa.org/research/action/romantic-relationships.aspx)

---

[2]There is not a lot of teenager-friendly information out there about polyandry and dating, but here is a little introduction: http://www.scarleteen.com/article/in_your_own_words/polyamorous_does_that_mean_you_like_parrots_0

with views and comments. The premise of her post is one that has been used lots of times by people trying to talk about consent, but her post was the one that took off, got a ton  of responses, and has become a standard for talking about consent. Here is that post, reprinted in the exact form it was originally written (or, if you'd rather, there's an amusing narrated animation that recreates this post, which you can watch here: https://vimeo.com/126553913):

Consent: Not Actually That Complicated[1]

If you're still struggling, just imagine instead of initiating sex, you're making them a cup of tea.

You say "hey, would you like a cup of tea?" and they go "omg fuck yes, I would fucking LOVE a cup of tea! Thank you!" then you know they want a cup of tea.

If you say "hey, would you like a cup of tea?" and they um and ahh and say, "I'm not really sure . . . " then you can make them a cup of tea or not, but be aware that they might not drink it, and if they don't drink it then—this is the important bit—*don't make them drink it*. You can't blame them for you going to the effort of making the tea on the off-chance they wanted it; you just have to deal with them not drinking it. Just because you made it doesn't mean you are entitled to watch them drink it.

If they say "No thank you," then don't make them tea. At all. Don't make them tea, don't make them drink tea, don't get annoyed at them for not wanting tea. They just don't want tea, okay?

They might say "Yes please, that's kind of you," and then when the tea arrives, they actually don't want the tea at all. Sure, that's kind of annoying as you've gone to the effort of making the tea, but they remain under no obligation to drink the tea. They did want tea, now they don't. Sometimes people change their mind in the time it takes to boil that kettle, brew the tea, and add the milk. And it's okay for people to change their mind, and you are still not entitled to watch them drink it even though you went to the trouble of making it.

If they are unconscious, don't make them tea. Unconscious people don't want tea and can't answer the question "do you want tea," because they are *unconscious*.

Okay, maybe they were conscious when you asked them if they wanted tea, and they said yes, but in the time it took you to boil that kettle, brew the tea, and add the milk, they are now unconscious. You should just put the tea down, make sure the unconscious person is safe, and—this is the important bit—don't make them drink the tea. They said yes then, sure, but unconscious people don't want tea.

If someone said yes to tea, started drinking it, and then passed out before they'd finished it, don't keep on pouring it down their throat. Take the tea away and make sure they are safe. Because *unconscious people don't want tea.* Trust me on this.

If someone said yes to tea around your house last Saturday, that doesn't mean that they want you to make them tea all the time. They don't want you to come around unexpectedly to their place and make them tea and force them to drink it going "BUT YOU WANTED TEA LAST WEEK," or to wake up to find you pouring tea down their throat going "BUT YOU WANTED TEA LAST NIGHT."

Do you think this is a stupid analogy? Yes, you all know this already—of course, you wouldn't force feed someone tea because they said yes to a cup last week. Of COURSE, you wouldn't pour tea down the throat of an unconscious person because they said yes to tea five minutes ago when they were conscious. But if you can understand how completely ludicrous it is to force people to have tea when they don't want tea, and you are able to understand when people don't want tea, then how hard is it to understand when it comes to sex?

Whether it's tea or sex, Consent Is Everything.

And on that note, I am going to make myself a cup of tea.

There are lots of things that the post and video got right and a few things that the post and video missed. Before I talk about them, I hope that you'll think over your own thoughts and reactions with these questions:

Consent and Tea Q's

1. Did the blog/video explain consent in a way that you could understand it? What points were useful?

2. Did the blog/video explain consent in a way that you think it would be useful to other people? How would you explain them?

3. How is consenting to drink tea like consenting to have sex? What did the blog/video get right?

4. How is consenting to drink to not like consenting to have sex? What did the blog/video get wrong?

Now that you've thought about your own reactions to the video, here are some of the things that other people think about it.

Pros

- Simple, easy to understand directions that take complex ideas and make them seem obvious. (Example: "Unconscious people don't want tea.")

- Amusing and accessible language that presents a hard topic in a way that lots of people can listen to and understand.

Cons

- Comparing consent *and tea* to consent *and sex* makes light of a complex and emotional issue.

- Most people who have sex with unconscious people do it because they don't care if the person consents, not because they are unaware that someone who is unconscious can't consent.

- Consent is complicated and can't be boiled down to a few lines.

- Rape can happen in many ways other than when someone is unconscious, and this video doesn't address those.

I'm going to be upfront about my biases. I like this post/video. I think the idea is accessible and fun and makes some awesome points. But, I also think it can't be used without other conversations about sexual consent. So, while it's a great place to start, we have to keep the dialogue going for it to be an effective conversation.

Types of Consent

Sexual consent is complex and sometimes it's confusing. Here are two examples of when it is hard to tell whether someone has consented to sexual contact:

Sarah likes to text Kris about all of the things that she's thinking and feeling and seeing, and sometimes she sends sexy pictures of herself. Kris doesn't usually text back. One day, Sarah asks Kris when they're at school if it's okay that she texts a lot. Kris doesn't answer the question, and asks what Sarah is having for lunch that day. Sarah starts talking about her leftovers from dinner last night. Sarah continued to text Kris often, even though Kris stopped replying at all.

One Friday night, Sarah texts Adrien and says her parents aren't home and asks Adrien to come over. Adrien shows up about an hour later and the two start kissing. Sarah takes her shirt off and starts to unbutton Adrien's pants. Adrien pushes Sarah's hands away and then starts to feel Sarah's breasts. Sarah is happy and enjoying herself and starts to unbutton Adrien's pants again. When Adrien pushes Sarah away again, Sarah says, "Oh, come on! We've gotten so close so many times before! What are all of the people at school going to say if I tell them that you didn't want to do this after all of

The Legal and the Social

There are both legal and social implications when we talk about sexual harassment, assault, and rape. The legal arena is relevant because sexual harassment, assault, and rape are all illegal. However, many people are unclear on what exactly it means for them to be illegal. The social arena is relevant because these things are painful social experiences that our culture doesn't respond to effectively or compassionately. Sexual harassment happens in ways that the law doesn't address or restrict. Harassment, assault, and rape are rarely prosecuted. While the law might say that you can't harass, assault, or rape someone without punishment, the reality of our culture is that people do these things and aren't punished. Sometimes, in fact, they are outwardly supported and treated as victims for being accused of harassment or rape, even when there is ample evidence that they sexually harmed another person. The reality is that our culture, our friends and family, and our legal system all respond to sexual violence in complex ways. While I will be parsing these issues out to some degree, there will be much left unexplored. I hope you will take the time to look through the resources listed throughout and at the end of this chapter. They are so important to a deeper understanding of the issue of consent and lack of consent.

You Have Rights

You have the right to not be touched in ways that you have not consented to. You have the right for your educational and professional life to be free from unwanted conversations about sex and sexuality. In fact, you have many rights when it comes to sex and sexuality. The World Association of Sexual Health (WAS) says that all human beings have sexual rights. Here are a few that are relevant to the conversation about consent:

- **The right to autonomy and bodily integrity.** (Which means you have the right to make all of the decisions about your own body.)

- **The right to be free from all forms of violence and coercion.** (Which means no one can tell you what to do or force you into anything sexual.)

- **The right to the highest attainable standard of health, including sexual health; with the possibility of pleasurable, satisfying, and safe sexual experiences.** (Which means you are able to be sexually healthy in a physical sense, and you have the option of having sexual pleasure.)

- **The right to enter, form, and dissolve marriage and other similar types of relationships based on equality and full and free consent.** (Which means you can choose which sexual and romantic relationships you want to be in without anyone else forcing or manipulating you into or out of those relationships.)

- **The right to access justice, remedies, and redress.** (Which means you are able to take legal actions against someone who has violated your sexual rights.)

WAS's Declaration of Sexual Rights has not been ratified by the United States, which means it is not part of our legal system. It is too bad that we haven't adopted it, because those things *should be* included in our country's Bill of Rights. While our laws suggest that some of the sexual rights, like the access to justice, remedies, and redress, should be accessible, they are not always. Our cultural perception of these issues overrides the legal ones because it is ultimately people from our culture who administer our laws. If a lawyer, judge, or member of a jury believes a woman was raped, likely because she was wearing something that showed too much skin or had led the other person on or that it was her fault for some other reason, they will put her on trial for her behavior, rather than the person who raped her.

While knowing your legal and moral rights is important, it does not mean that you will never have those rights breached. There is a section at the end of this chapter about responding to and healing from sexual violence—both for yourself and for you to use in support of friends and family.

If It Feels Gross, It's Not Okay

You can apply the title of this section to pretty much all aspects of life, but in this chapter, it applies to the ways that people talk about sexuality around and to you and the ways that you are touched. Sexual harassment, specifically, is frequently misunderstood. Sexual harassment in the workplace, which is the only place many people think it is a problem, is illegal. Here is the legal definition:

Unwelcome sexual advances, requests for sexual favors, and other verbal or physical conduct of a sexual nature constitute sexual harassment when:
- *Submission to such conduct is made either explicitly or implicitly a term or condition of an individual's employment,*
- *Submission to or rejection of such conduct by an individual is used as the basis for employment decisions affecting such individuals, or*
- *Such conduct has the purpose or effect of unreasonably interfering with an individual's work performance or creating an intimidating, hostile, or offensive working environment. (29 C.F.R. §1604.11 [1980])*

Sexual harassment is also illegal in school environments, so let's read that definition, too. The US Department of Education defines sexual harassment in the following way:

Sexual harassment is conduct that:

1. is sexual in nature;

2. is unwelcome; and

3. denies or limits a student's ability to participate in or benefit from a school's education program.

So you just avoid those things! Easy peasy, right?

Well, not so much. Much of the complex nature of understanding sexual harassment comes from the word "unwelcome" that exists in both the workplace and the school definitions. That word refers to the person who is on the receiving end of behavior, or is even just observing the behavior, and is the one who determines whether or not it is sexual harassment. For example, if two people are consensually flirting in a classroom and one of them brushes the other's hair out of their eyes and then lets their finger trail down their neck, that can be a fun and sexy interaction. If someone doesn't want their hair pushed out of their eyes or someone's finger trailing down their neck, it could feel extremely invasive, and absolutely be sexual harassment. The difference is not in the specific actions of the person who is brushing the hair, but in the perception of the person whose hair is being brushed.

For something to be defined as sexual harassment, it also needs to be either consistent or extreme or some combination of consistent and extreme. Some examples to explain what this means:

- If someone asks you out on a date, that is a one-time, low-level exploration of interest and doesn't qualify as sexual harassment.

- If someone asks you out on a date and you say no, and they continue to ask you, and you continue to say no, every day for a month, that becomes sexual harassment because while every interaction is low level, the frequency makes it reach a threshold to be considered harassment.

- If someone tells you that you have to go on a date with them, whether you want to or not, that is sexual harassment because it is high level, even though it only happened one time.

If you're experiencing sexual harassment at work or school, knowing how to reach out, who to reach out to, how to talk about it, and how to get the protection that you have a legal and moral right to is not always clear and is rarely easy. It is, however, something to remember that you DO have a right to. Finding the person who you feel is likely to be the most supportive of you and asking them to talk with you privately is the best first step. That person might be a friend or family member, a teacher or someone you work with, a therapist or a clergy member. Ideally, the person is supportive of you emotionally and has an understanding of what sexual harassment is and how to support someone (like you!) who is being harassed.

When steps are made to stop or prevent sexual harassment, remember that the person who is being harassed should not have to change their behavior. They are not the ones who need to change their class or work schedule or how they dress. The person who is the harasser needs to change their behavior, possibly including their class or work schedule.

their will. Hopefully it won't take another 85 years for this definition to be revised and improved.

The US cultural perspectives around rape are so backward and confusing, so deeply entrenched in rape culture, that it is difficult to properly discuss those issues in one section in a book like this. What comes next are a few of the biggest issues surrounding rape, including accessing legal help, moving forward emotionally and sexually, and the ways that rape culture hides the realities of rape. If you have questions or concerns that go beyond what is covered here, the resources at the end of this chapter are rich in their depth. This chapter is merely a primer on discussing these emotional issues.

Reporting

Rape is one of the most under-reported crimes in the US. More rapes happen without being reported than any other crime. The reason why makes sense: People believe you when you say that your house was burglarized, but people are less likely to believe you if you say you were raped. One of the primary reasons for this is that three-fourths of rapes are by someone who the victim knows. Many people, upon hearing that someone was raped by a friend, wrongly believe that they must have wanted to it in the moment because why would a friend take advantage of them? Reporting the rape means reporting a friend, family member, or acquaintance as having hurt you on a very intimate level. In fact, two-thirds of all rapes are NOT reported to the police. Even more rapes are dismissed or ignored by police and judges. With so few reports being made and taken seriously, few people are willing to take the social and emotional risk of reporting a rape or sexual assault. It is important, however, that you report when and if you are able, while maintaining your own sexual, physical, and emotional safety. Increased reports of rape have the possibility of increasing awareness and improving response by the entire legal system, from the police to the District Attorney.

If you decide that you are able to report a rape or a sexual assault, don't do it alone. Have your support network on call, and ideally with you, to provide you with emotional support during a difficult process.

Even in the best of environments, recalling and reporting a violation as extreme as rape and sexual assault is an emotional and difficult process. Having someone whom you love and trust to take care of you in the way(s) that you want to be cared for is critical during the process.

Moving Forward From Assault and Rape

If you have been raped or sexually assaulted, whether or not you decide to report it, you will need to find a way to process your experience and move forward. For some people, the reporting itself is a first step toward healing. For other people, it only makes the experience more painful. You may not know how you will react or feel until you've started down one path or the other. Over time, you may try a number of different approaches to healing. For example, some people need silence and privacy, while other people need their community, and you might find that sometimes people need a combination of both. Accept your process as unpredictable, but move along with it. Let yourself need what you need when you need it without being judgmental of yourself.

The amount of time it will take to begin a healing process also varies, and sometimes varies dramatically. The specifics of your experience will likely impact your path toward healing, with a deeper physical and emotional toll often being the result of, for example, ongoing assault or rape, or experiencing assault and rape as a child, and other ways involving higher levels of emotional, physical, and identity-related pain. Allow yourself space to move toward healing without expecting it to happen on a certain timeline. Those expectations can slow down the process because you think it should look like something else.

Many people need support and help, not only from their friends, but also from professionals. You can get help online, 24/7, by visiting https://hotline.rainn.org/online or by calling 800-656-HOPE (4673).

You are not alone. You do not have to be alone. There are people who can help, and you have access to them.

What Rape Culture Means

Our culture is grounded in untrue assumptions about rape, including assumptions about a certain kind of person being more likely to be raped because of the choices they are making. These assumptions are the essence of rape culture. The following are truths that can be used to combat myths about rape and sexual assault.

- People of all genders can be sexually harassed, assaulted, and raped, including people with penises.

- People can experience sexual arousal and even orgasm during a rape. That doesn't mean that they wanted it to happen, that they enjoyed it, or that the trauma is any less deep.

- People with uteruses cannot prevent a pregnancy from happening during a rape.

- Seventy-five percent of people who are raped are raped by people they know.

- Just because a person's physical safety or life wasn't threatened, doesn't mean it wasn't rape. There are psychological and emotional ways to control someone that can be just as damaging as physical violence.

- Being drunk, wearing revealing clothing, and flirting are never forms of consent to sexual contact.

- Yes, even if someone was flirting and kissing, they haven't consented to either continued or more intimate levels of sexual contact.

- You never, ever owe anyone sexual contact for any reason.

- Sexual consent can be withdrawn at any time, at which point all sexual contact must stop.

Living in a rape culture means that many people believe the opposite of each of those things. I have found that people may be able to see these truths about rape when they are *presented* in a theoretical sense. However, when they are *experienced*, seeing them as truths becomes more difficult. When a person who you respect and love breaches your sexual boundaries, the striking difference between the ways that you expect them to act and the ways that they are actually acting becomes hard to see and understand.

This is what rape culture can do to people: It can gaslight us. It can make us doubt our own experiences. Hopefully, by knowing this to be true, you will be able to fight against that tide and believe your own intuition about your sexual experiences, both good and bad.

Additional Resources

Rape, Abuse, & Incest National Network (RAINN) (https://rainn.org/)

Yes Means Yes!: Visions of Female Sexual Power and a World Without Rape by Jaclyn Friedman and Jessica Valenti. (2008).

Yes Means Yes (http://www.yesmeansyes.com/)

"10 Lies We're Told About Rape Survivors" on Everyday Feminism (http://everydayfeminism.com/2016/05/lies-told-about-rape-survivors/)

might be wrong. Most of the time, if the penetration is something that the person wants to be doing, pain happens because the penetration happened too quickly or without enough lubricant. If using water-based lubricant and going more slowly doesn't address the issue, it might be that the penis or sex toy is too large for the person being penetrated in the position that they are in. Try changing position; when the person being penetrated is the one on top, they have more control over depth and speed, which makes it far less likely that they will experience pain. If they're using a sex toy, they can try penetration with something smaller than what they were initially using. If they want to have penetrative sex with a penis, but the penis hurts, they could try using a finger first and then slowly building up to two fingers and eventually a penis. If they've tried everything, and it still hurts, they might want to make an appointment with a gynecologist to rule out infections or other issues.

You have the moral and ethical right to control your body and the kinds of pleasure and pain that you choose to feel. You do not have to be in pain to have good or satisfying sexual experiences.

First Time Q's

1. Are you worried that it will hurt the first time you are penetrated?

2. How can you talk with your partner about reducing or eliminating the pain?

First Time Ever

From the first time you kiss someone to the first time you sexually touch someone's naked body to the first time that you experiment with a kink or fetish (see more on kinks and fetishes in Chapter 20), all of your sexual experiences have the potential to be exciting, sexy, and filled with laughter, pleasure, and mutuality. While many people consider the first kiss and the first time having penetrative sex to be the most important firsts, there are so many more! You might continue to have firsts throughout your entire sexual life if you and your partner(s) are experimental and enjoy trying new things. Too many adults consider their days of sexual firsts to be over and done with. They consider it something they did as teenagers and now they forget that firsts are still possible. But they *are* still possible! And so, if you have already had penetrative sex, this section is still for you. I have no doubt that you have more sexual firsts ahead of you.

There are a few things that help firsts to be fun and feel good and these apply regardless of what the first is—whether it's a kiss or being penetrated or another sexual activity. One part of doing a first is that you're taking care of your physical, sexual, and emotional self. It also means you're taking care of your partner's physical, sexual, and emotional self.

Here are a few things related to consent and physical and sexual safety that you should do when considering a sexual first:

- Decide that you want to do the activity.

- Read up on it. Learn what you need to know to do it as safely as possible. There is almost always some risk with sexual activities, including penile-vaginal intercourse, even with condoms. Condoms and other barrier methods are effective, reliable, and relatively low-cost risk reduction methods that should always be in your safer sex toolkit.

- Talk with your partner about what it is that you want to do and find out if they want to do it too.

- Talk with your partner about how you can reduce the risks and increase the fun of the activity.

The benefits of being knowledgeable and communicative with your partner cannot be overstated!

above are not things that all people must do at all times, but rather are ways to reduce the emotional, physical, and sexual risks involved in sexual intercourse. If you choose to engage in sexual activity that is higher risk, you need to know that is what you are doing and actively choose it, rather than accidentally putting yourself at risk because you lacked information.

First Time Ever Q's

1. Is there anything that you feel is important to do before you have sex for the first time that is not included in the lists above?

2. Is there anything in the lists above that you think is not important to do before you have sex for the first time?

3. How would you feel if your potential partner didn't want to talk with you about sex before you had sex for the first time?

4. What might you say to your partner if they didn't want to talk with you about sex?

New Partner Firsts

This section, like the last section, isn't only for people who haven't had penetrative sex yet (if you have had sex, and so you skipped it, go back and read it!). If you've kissed someone before and are thinking about kissing a new person now, this section is for you. If you think you're going to kiss more than one person at some point in your life, this section is for you. If you have friends who come to you and talk with you about their experiences kissing or having sex, this section is for you.

If you take only one thing from this section, I hope it is this: Because you have done
a certain sexual act with someone in the
past does not mean you have to do it ever
again. With the same person or with anyone else, you can say no. You can stop it
part way through. You can say no.

But let's assume that you're excited about trying something with
a new partner that you've done before with someone else. Maybe that
something is kissing, maybe it's oral sex, maybe something entirely different. You still need to think and talk about the risks and the benefits
and whether you and your potential partner are both excited about being together in this specific way. You may feel like doing this thing with a
new person is lower stakes because you've done it before with someone
else. But the risk doesn't go away just because you've done it before.

Sexual activities can be seen on a spectrum—from light, low-risk
touching (like holding someone's hand) to very intimate, high-risk
touching (like penetrative sex). The first few times you hold someone's
hand, you might have been (or might in the future be) nervous about
it. And the first time that you hold a new person's hand might be exciting for its newness—but it may not be something that you lose a
lot of sleep over or call your friends to gush about. However, penetrative sex is something that you are more likely to talk with your friends
about when you have a brand new partner. This is an indication of the
difference between the two kinds of touch. I don't want to suggest
that holding hands with someone will never be friend-gossip-worthy,
because it very well might be. Just that it's less likely to be.

Even after you've had sex for the first time, you should still go
through the steps in this chapter when you're deciding to have sex
with someone new. However, there is one notable difference: Getting
tested for STIs. If you or your partner have been sexual with another
person, you should both get tested before you exchange fluids or are
fluid bonded.

Getting tested together is a nice habit to put in place with each
new partner as you increase your physical, emotional, and sexual con-

and it will most likely be people with vaginas who feel that way—is because of a sexual build-up leading to ejaculation. There is more information on female ejaculation in a section further along in this chapter.

Orgasm Feeling Q's

1. If you have experienced an orgasm, what do your orgasms feel like? Make your language as expressive as possible!

2. If you have a friend whom you can talk with about sex, ask them what their orgasms feel like. What do they say?

3. What are the best parts of orgasming alone? (If you haven't had this experience, what do you think they might be?)

4. What are the best parts of orgasming with a partner? (If you haven't had this experience, what do you think they might be?)

The Biology of the Orgasm

Now for some biology details: An orgasm is a rhythmic contracting of many of the muscles involved in sexual reproduction, including:

- internal and external clitoris
- vaginal walls
- bladder
- rectum
- penis

- prostate

- and a few more

 Note: Need a primer on all of those organs? Head back to Chapter 4 for a minute and take a look at the diagrams on pp. 70–72 or head to the Anatomy Glossary at the end of the book.

The contractions usually feel really good. They can last anywhere from a few seconds to much longer.

What comes before, during, and after those rhythmic contractions depends very much on the person, their body, their brain, and their arousal cycle. (Details on the arousal cycle are also in Chapter 4.) The fact of the matter is that what moves any individual person to orgasm is very unique, both biologically and emotionally. However, let's clear up one big issue: Most people with vaginas do not orgasm through vaginal penetration alone. It is almost always the internal and/or external clitoris that is involved in female orgasm. The penis is the other part of sexual anatomy that is most commonly associated with the biology of experiencing an orgasm. But clitorises and penises aren't the only body parts that can experience orgasm. For some people, kissing their ears, sucking on their nipples, and even just thinking about orgasming can bring them to orgasm. Some people orgasm when they exercise! All of this is to say, it's worth exploring by yourself at first and with a partner as you know yourself better to see what feels good to you. It might be that what feels good to you will evolve over time, so the exploration is something that will continue over time. Chapter 22 has more about being sexual throughout your life.

Stimulation of the clitoris—rather than stimulation of the vagina—is very important to most people with clitorises—rather than stimulation of the vagina. The vagina doesn't actually have many nerve endings in it, and most vaginal stimulation is actually stimulating the internal clitoris. Whether vaginal penetration, and particularly penile-vaginal orgasm—orgasming through vaginal penetration alone—as the best, most desirable orgasm. But it's not. You might be wondering why this question is addressed in the psychology section rather than the biology section. So here's a short history of the vaginal/clitoral divide that has become so prevalent in our understandings about the orgasm:

Sigmund Freud is the father of modern therapy. He was a psychologist before psychologists really existed. Freud was the first one to talk about a difference between a clitoral and a vaginal orgasm. While Freud offered a lot to the field of psychology, he made it very clear that he did not understand women. Nevertheless, Freud made bold statements about women's sexuality. He was the first to say that the clitoral orgasm is a "childish" orgasm, and that the vaginal orgasm is a "mature" orgasm. Given the very limited understanding of the anatomy involved in orgasms associated with the clitoris or the vagina when Freud was alive, it's not surprising how wrong he was. In fact, regardless of where the sexual stimulation comes from, the biology of the orgasm remains the same. It may feel different, depending on a number of factors like whether there is anything penetrating the vagina at the time of orgasm. Some people experience a deeper, more pleasurable orgasm during vaginal penetration because of a physical preference for the sensations of their vaginal walls pushing against something inside their vaginas *and* a psychological enjoyment of being penetrated. In other words, it's not all biological.

The experience of orgasm is absolutely connected with a person's psychological belief structures. For example, when a person feels like they cannot orgasm or is distracted or worried, their emotional state often negatively impacts their potential to orgasm. Even when there is nothing physically stopping a person from orgasming, their psychological or emotional state can stop them. This is true for people regardless of their anatomy. Sexual pleasure is deeply tied to the ways that people perceive themselves, their bodies, and the desirability of their own orgasms.

The Culture of the Orgasm

People who are treated like girls and women may be taught that their orgasms, while perhaps nice, are not necessary and may be considered time consuming or bothersome to their partners. People who are treated like boys and men may be taught that their orgasms are an indication of power and are necessary and worthy of the attention of their partners. This kind of cultural perception, whether a person overtly believes it or they have it in the back of their mind without really paying attention to it, can have a substantial impact on how someone feels about their sexual pleasure and to what degree they experience orgasms. Critically examining your own thought process and emotions and preconceptions about your anatomy and its orgasmic process is useful. It can give you an opportunity to consider what sexual and orgasmic potential you might have and to stabilize and improve your psychological self-perception.

In addition to gendered understandings of orgasms, our culture gives value to orgasm in many different ways. It can function as a relationship tally, if a partner keeps track of who's had more. Or it can be used as a judge of how good someone is at having sex, based on whether or not a partner experiences orgasm with them. It can be a marker of what someone likes sexually, based on what they like to do when they experience orgasm. Sometimes it can even be a point of personal shame, if someone worries about how long they take to orgasm or what kind of stimulation they need.

All of these things are cultural in nature and do not necessarily serve us as individuals or as partners in a sexual relationship. They are built on our culture's assumptions about sexuality and relationships and identity, not on your sexual or romantic reality. The way that you integrate cultural assumptions into your relationships is entirely up to you and your partner.

Your orgasm is your own. If you relinquish cultural assumptions about orgasms in general, your experience and feelings can become even more your own. The same is also true for your partner—their orgasm is uniquely theirs and they can be responsible for their own feelings of sexual pleasure and orgasm. If you and your partner take control over your own feelings of pleasure and capacities to orgasm, you will both gain a lot in your sexual relationship.

Each person taking ownership of their own pleasure does not mean that you won't touch each other or that you won't bring each other to orgasm. Rather, it means that you can and will touch each other *and* yourselves during your sexual activities. It means that you will be honest and communicative with each other about what feels good and what may bring you to orgasm. It means a shared responsibility. If you decide to work together in these ways on shared sexual experiences, building on your individual experiences, you can create something new and beautiful and pleasurable. You can come together in a way where each person acknowledges and enjoys the uniqueness of their own and the other person's experiences of sexual pleasure. While this is not a culturally common representation of sexual activities and orgasm, it is one that most people find far more pleasurable and exciting than the common approach of each person being entirely responsible for the other person's orgasm.

Orgasm Culture Q's

1. What did you learn about orgasms when you were young?

2. If you didn't learn anything about orgasms, why do you think that was?

3. If you did learn things about orgasms, was the information accurate?

4. What do you think people need to know about orgasms and at what age should they learn it?

Managing Orgasms

There are so many ways that people worry about their orgasms and want to have control over them; they may worry that they come too fast, too long, too loud, not at all, with pain, etc. There are so many concerns that pop up because of cultural assumptions about what an orgasm "should" be. People want to have control over them. Some orgasms are more easily controlled than others. For example, for a person who orgasms too quickly, which is more commonly a problem for people with penises, teaching their body to slow down by masturbating almost to the point of orgasm and then backing off over and over again can often make the orgasms take longer. This is something that is relatively easy to do alone with little guidance. However, if you experience pain during penetration or orgasm, which is more commonly a problem for people with vaginas, there are techniques that help, but they are usually more effective when done with a therapist who understands sexuality and sexual pain. To address substantial and ongoing vaginal pain, a therapist will usually support the person masturbating and penetrating themselves beginning with very small tools, or even just touching their vulva without penetration. This helps the vaginal walls to learn that genital touching and vaginal penetration can be pleasurable and that they can relax rather than seize up.

But what if you don't orgasm? Or your partner doesn't orgasm? This can be a huge problem in a sexual relationship. It can make you or your partner feel like a bad lover, which is never a relationship bonus. There is not one fix for experiencing orgasms. Instead, it usually takes time, trying out different kinds of touch, talking with your partner, taking things slowly, and a desire to find a solution. While it may seem hit-or-miss, someone experienced in supporting people who are anorgasmic (unable to have an orgasm), like an American Association of Sexuality Educators, Counselors, and Therapists (AASECT) certified therapist or educator will have a list of things to try out and is often helpful to talk with. The most important thing is to rely on communication and honesty with your partner, so that you both know what the other person wants and is comfortable with.

Ejaculations and Orgasms

There's an assumption that when a penis orgasms there is an ejaculation involved, but that when a vagina orgasms there's not. While this may be true for many people and their orgasms, it's not true for every person or every situation.

Let's talk about vaginas that ejaculate first. The fluid that is sometimes expelled from a vagina before or during an orgasm has very different properties when compared to the fluid that is expelled from a penis during orgasm. The most obvious difference is the fact that vaginal ejaculate doesn't have any sperm in it and has no way of getting someone pregnant. There are other differences as well, but medical research has been mostly silent on the exact make-up of vaginal ejaculate. There appear to be trace levels of urine, but it is not mostly urine. Similarly, there are trace levels of vaginal lubrication, but it is not mostly lubrication. Vaginal ejaculations sometimes occur at the same time as the orgasm, but not always.

There is, obviously, a lot that we don't know about vaginal ejaculations. What are things that we do know? Well, we know that it is more likely for a vagina to ejaculate if the g-spot has been stimulated, but this is not the only time or way. We know that when a person's vagina is about to ejaculate, they often feel a buildup of pressure suggesting they need to pee. We know some vaginas are more likely to ejaculate than others. The information about vaginal ejaculations will likely continue to increase as interest in it grows, but as of the writing of this book, that's about all we have.

When a vagina unexpectedly ejaculates, it can be surprising for both the ejaculator and their partner. However, it is often something people want to experience. If experiencing an ejaculation is something you or your partner is excited about trying to do, g-spot stimulation is the place to start. However, it is not always possible for a person with a vagina to ejaculate. Particularly if it becomes something that the couple is focusing on over everything else—that can detract from the sexual experience and the possibility of experiencing any kind of orgasm.

People often assume that vaginas never ejaculate and penises always ejaculate. However, sometimes penises do not ejaculate with orgasm. I would like to point out that relying on non-ejaculating orgasms is a poor approach to birth control. Sometimes when a penis orgasms without ejaculation, it is an indication of a medical condition called retrograde ejaculation where the ejaculation goes into the bladder rather than out of the penis. This is not necessarily a medical problem in and of itself unless it is uncomfortable or the couple is hoping to get pregnant. A person with a penis can also learn how to have orgasms without ejaculations in order to have multiple orgasms. This comes naturally for some people with penises; for others it's a learned skill.

And What ABOUT Multiples?

Multiple orgasms! Many people with vaginas can experience multiple orgasms, which basically means two or more orgasms one after the other. For some people this feels like an orgasm that peaks and then slows down and then another orgasm. For others it feels more like a really long orgasm. Often the intensity of the orgasms increases as the number increases. Many people find this to be a fun perk when it happens.

Many people with penises experience something called a refractory period, which was briefly addressed in Chapter 4. The refractory period means that a penis is flaccid and can't get erect for a period of time after ejaculation. The refractory period lengthens over the lifespan for many people from being shorter as a teenager to being much longer as an older adult. The refractory period is why people with penises are less likely to be able to have multiple orgasms because their orgasmic ability usually depends on having an erect penis. However, the refractory period only comes after an ejaculation. This is why learning to experience orgasm without an ejaculation allows for people with penises to have multiple orgasms.

How Do You Know If Your Partner Has Had an Orgasm??

So many people worry about this—especially people who have sex

Chapter 17

Masturbation

Why is masturbation a thing? This chapter explains how and why people masturbate, discussing anatomy and pleasure, and dispelling the myths around masturbation.

Masturbation Is Great!

There are some really good things that masturbation can bring to someone's life, including:

- an increased knowledge of their own body,
- a stronger immune system,
- better sleeping patterns,
- a more relaxed mood,
- more sexual pleasure both alone and with a future partner,
- and no risk of STIs or pregnancy!

While there are so many good things that come from masturbation, that doesn't mean everyone loves doing it. There are lots of different perspectives that people may have about masturbation. For example, some people:

- Love it!
- Don't want to masturbate.
- Worry that masturbation would be gross or scary.
- Enjoys masturbation at night before sleep.
- Think that masturbation will ruin sex with a partner.

• Feel guilty about masturbation.

• Like to masturbate with a partner.

It is important to know your own body, and one of masturbation's biggest perks is that it can help you do that. However, there is no reason to masturbate if you don't want to or don't enjoy it. But it's good to try it at least a few times to find out if it's for you and to get to know your body a little better.

For something that is usually done alone, masturbation draws a lot of attention, thought, and concern. In fact, it was the only topic that *all* of the youth and young adult writers for this book wanted to contribute diary entries about. So you'll notice that they all have something to say in this chapter, giving you a broad range of perspectives on the topic.

While opinions are one thing, and of course, everyone has their own opinions and preferences about masturbation, the facts are a different matter. Many people are unclear on the details of masturbation. When myths inform someone's sexuality, they can make mistakes, put themselves at increased risk, and narrow their options unnecessarily, so it is critical to know the facts about all aspects of sexuality, including masturbation.

Myths and Truths

Here are a few of the myths that people have believed about masturbation and the truth behind them:

Myth	Truth
Masturbation will make you go blind.	Masturbation has no impact on eyesight. The only possible effect of masturbation on eyesight might be a slight stinging if you were to ejaculate into your eye, but it's not going to blind you. Well, if you are infected with an STI and you ejaculate into your or someone else's eye, it's possible to contract gonorrhea or syphilis or herpes of the eye. And it's possible that if left untreated, the eye could go blind. Therefore, if you masturbate and your ejaculate gets in your eye and you have any question about your STI status, you should get yourself tested.

Myth	Truth
If you masturbate, you'll grow hair on the palms of your hands.	Touching your pubic hair will not, ever, transplant the pubic hair onto your hands. Never. Where did this myth even come from?
If you masturbate too much, having sex with a partner won't be fun or pleasurable.	Masturbation can teach you what feels good to you, which makes partnered sex even more fun because you can share this info with your partner. However, if you masturbate a lot and in only one way, that can reduce the likelihood that you will orgasm through other kinds of stimulation, like the ways that your partner might touch you. To avoid this, touch yourself in different ways when you masturbate. If you find that you've gotten into a masturbation habit, mix it up.
If you masturbate too much, you won't be able to fall in love with a partner because you'll have fallen in love with yourself in that way.	If every time someone had sex they fell in love, the world would be a very different place. However, falling in love with someone is an entirely different phenomenon than being accepting, compassionate, and loving toward yourself. But if masturbation leads to being accepting, compassionate, and loving toward yourself, those are just three more things that would make it a good idea rather than a bad idea. Masturbation does not keep a person from falling in love with someone else.
Masturbation is addictive.	Sex, including both masturbation and partnered sex, can be really, really fun and some people want to do it so often that it interferes with them having a balanced life. Some people may feel out of control about how often they masturbate. However, masturbation and sex are not addictive, according to a medical definition of addiction. Still, sometimes people do need help to stop masturbating as much so that they can still have full, engaging lives. More the issue of addiction in Chapter 20.
If you masturbate, it's because you've been abused or have something wrong with you.	Nope. Most people masturbate because it is fun!

People with penises usually touch their penis during masturbation. Many people enjoy stroking the penis up and down. The genitals near the penis also feel good when touched, and so the testicles, scrotum, and prostate may be included in masturbation. The prostate is stimulated through penetration of the anus, which is why many people with penises enjoy when their partner puts a finger, penis, or a sex toy into their anus.

For people who are intersex, masturbation can include any and all of the above, depending on what the person finds pleasurable.

Usually, but not always, the things that feel good during masturbation are the things that feel good during partnered sex. While there are a few ways that people can't touch themselves like their partners can (very few people can perform oral sex on themselves, for example), one of the reasons that masturbation is useful is because it teaches you what kinds of touch your body responds to. The same is true in reverse: If there is a certain way that your partner touches you during sex, you may enjoy touching yourself that way when you are masturbating.

Are There Any Safety Concerns With Masturbation?

The good news is that there aren't any safety concerns about STI transmission or unplanned pregnancies! However, there are a few important things to remember about how to masturbate safely. The same three issues also apply to partnered sex.

- If you want to use a sex toy, like a vibrator or a dildo, buy one from a sex toy store (or online) that is designed for that purpose. Using a household item can put your sexual health at risk. There is more information about vibrators and dildos in Chapter 20.

- If you feel pleasure from anal stimulation, use a condom to cover anything you put into your anus, including your fingers. A very thorough washing might be used in place of a condom, but a condom is easier. The anus may house bacteria that could make you sick, even if there isn't an STI present.

- Do not move something from your anus to your vagina without putting on a new condom, for the same reason as above.

Other than these few issues, masturbation is very, very safe.

What If I Don't Want to Masturbate?

That's fine! Masturbation is a personal choice, and that choice can include deciding not to masturbate. People who don't masturbate say that they don't for a bunch of reasons, including their religion, that it doesn't feel sexy to them, that they don't have enough privacy, and that they just don't want to.

However, when teen girls feel hesitant or uncomfortable touching and interacting with their own bodies, it can be because someone has led them to believe that their bodies are gross or smelly or that it's wrong. This kind of sentiment is hurtful and says more about the person communicating it and their own body issues than anything about you and your body. Your body is your own to love, touch, and take care of. It's the only body you'll ever have, and getting to know it and taking care of it is important.

If you don't want to masturbate for any reason, that's fine. But be sure that it's about you, and not about someone else's belief about what's good or right for you.

What If I Want to Masturbate All the Time?

That may or may not be a problem; it really depends on what you mean by "all the time." Many things are good when they're part of a full and interesting life, but can be bad if you focus on them so much that you don't pay attention to anything else. Masturbation is no different. If you masturbate in bed every night as a way of relaxing and falling asleep, that's not a problem. If you masturbate several times every day and it keeps you from finishing your schoolwork or doing things with your family and friends, then that is a problem.

If you find that you often masturbate instead of doing other things, you may need to consider a healthier way to be sexual with yourself *and* still engage in other activities and with other people. Reaching out for help in this kind of situation can be emotionally difficult and finding the right kind of help for your specific needs can feel impossible, but it's not impossible. There is more information on what to do if you are feeling out of control sexually in Chapter 20.

Flirting

Flirting usually comes before any other kind of sexual connection. It can, and should, come after, too. This is the way that people express their interest in and, potentially, their specific desires for each other, and get a feel for the other person's interest. Flirting can be verbal and nonverbal; it includes everything from private texts to public social media messages to eye contact to the way you touch elbows. Flirting can be alluring, sensual, sexual, funny, and so many other things. It involves all of our senses and all of our attention.

While flirting at its best is fun and lighthearted, some people worry about it, especially if they are new to flirting. If you are worried about the way you flirt or communicate your sexual or romantic interest in another person, you're not alone. It's a point of concern for many people; I just did an internet search for "how to flirt" and got almost 100 million websites returned. That's a *lot* of advice on how someone should or could flirt. Here are some of the most common recommended flirting methods:

- Make eye contact

- Smile

- Touch the other person

- Compliment the other person

How you use these methods will depend on how well you know the other person and how obvious you want to be. Take making eye contact and smiling, for example. If you want to indicate your interest in someone new, you might let your eyes linger on them until they glance at you and then smile for a second longer than you otherwise would before you look away. If, however, you are flirting with someone you are in a sexual or romantic relationship with, you might look at them until they look at you, and then smile very slowly, maintaining eye contact for much longer. The same pattern is true of both touch and compliments. With someone you are just beginning to know you'll flirt and give them compliments that are not invasive to their personal space. If you have a standing relationship with someone, however, you might touch and compliment them in very personal and intimate ways as part of your flirtation.

These suggestions obviously can't apply when you're flirting by text or message. In situations where you are using text exclusively, you have to rely on things other than proximity and tone of voice to indicate interest. Emojis help with this. But it is easy to be confused about the exact intentions someone is trying to communicate when you have fewer context clues. Which is to say, while giving advice on flirting is easy, flirting itself is not easy.

When They Aren't Responding

If you are trying to flirt with someone you're interested in and they aren't giving you anything back, there's one of a few potential things happening:

1. **You aren't getting your point across.** Maybe you aren't even trying to flirt because you're shy or embarrassed, or maybe you aren't being obvious enough. Regardless of the situation, you need to up your flirtation game. If it's insecurities that are holding you back, try and remember that if you flirt and are rejected or the other person doesn't flirt back, their answer is that they are uninterested. It's clear and you can move on. But if you flirt, at least you have the potential to have your interest returned! If you are trying to flirt, but the other person doesn't notice, you might need to be a little more evident about your flirtations. Subtlety, by design, is not always obvious; you should be a little clearer so that the other person doesn't think you're just being friendly.

2. **The other person isn't paying attention.** It might be the case that you're a great flirter and no one has ever mistaken your flirtations for friendship. It might really be that the person you're trying to flirt with just isn't paying attention or doesn't have the social skills to notice what you're trying to do. Hopefully you know yourself and the person you're trying to flirt with well

Kissing

Kissing is something that many people experience from birth. Our parents, grandparents, siblings, and other family members kiss us in non-sexual ways. It is often one of our first sexual touches with a partner. Kissing seems so normal that writing so much about kissing may be a surprising idea. But because it is so intimately familiar and common, thinking more closely about our choices and habits and what does and doesn't feel good can have a dramatic and positive impact on our lives.

Kissing Q's

1. Have you ever told someone how you like to be kissed?

2. What would you say if someone who you wanted to kiss asked you if they could kiss you?

3. What is your favorite thing about kissing?

4. What is your least favorite thing about kissing?

5. What do you think kissing has to offer in a long-term relationship? What about a short-term relationship?

We learn how to do many concrete tasks from teachers or mentors, but this is not the case with most sexual touching—and even more rarely in the case of kissing. The reason why may become apparent if you do a quick Internet search for "how to kiss." As with flirting, more than 100 million pages come up, with many including pieces of advice like these:

- "Keep your slightly open mouth close to theirs and breathe in and out together." (http://www.bustle.com/articles/102354-how-to-kiss-someone-well-in-8-tongue-tying-steps)

- "Choose top or bottom; the more thickly fleshed is probably the best one. Once you've focused on just one lip, you create so many options: simple suction; the lip switch from top to bottom, or bottom to top; the sly addition of the tongue; escalation to a full-on frencher, then a teasing retreat; the nibble." (http://www.yourtango.com/20087725/how-to-kiss-well)

- " 'Listen' to the way she's kissing. Match her tempo. Reply to her tongue action with similar tongue action. Leading and being aggressive can be good but being oblivious is bad." (http://time.com/2800319/how-to-be-a-good-kisser-10-tips-from-scientific-research/)

- "Tilt your head to the right or left—if your partner is starting to tilt in one direction, you go the opposite way. This is so your noses don't collide before your lips do. If you can't tell which way the other person's gonna tilt, your best bet is to go right (meaning your right ear moves ever so slightly—like an inch or two—toward your right shoulder). I'd say most people go right like 95% of the time. (And if you make a miscalculation, just laugh it off and keep going.)" (http://www.rookiemag.com/2013/04/kissing-complete-guide/2/)

While none of this is bad advice, it is *a lot* of advice. It can feel overwhelming to try and keep it all in mind while you're trying to be intimate with someone. The *best* advice tends to be short and sweet, like this:

- Go slowly.

- Watch, listen, and feel for your partner's cues about what they like.

- Be playful.

- Have fun.

- Approach biting carefully.

the E is just right or whether the letters are upper or lower case, but what this does provide is the opportunity to stimulate the clitoris in many different ways to see what the other person responds to. Many people find that oral stimulation of the surrounding genitals, including the labia and the inside of the vagina, is also arousing and pleasurable.

Performing oral sex on a penis feels intimidating for many people. The penis, like the clitoris, is incredibly sensitive. For the most part, people with penises want them to be treated softly and with lots of lubrication. The usual lubrication during oral sex is saliva, which can be held in the mouth rather than swallowed or spit out onto the penis. Teeth are sometimes a big worry for people with a penis during oral sex, so their partners need to be attentive to that concern. Lips and tongues are usually the right level of soft and lubricated.

Regardless of the genitalia involved in oral sex, many people use their fingers and hands as part of the process. Just because it's called oral sex, doesn't mean that you shouldn't touch your partner at the same time. On a vulva, many people touch the vagina and the labia while they are orally stimulating the clitoris. On a penis, many people wrap their hand around the bottom part of the penis while they are orally stimulating the top of it. They may also touch, hold, or stroke the testicles. Regardless of the genitals, people may stroke or caress their partner's legs, butt, or torso, or hold their partner's hands during oral sex.

Many people worry about what to do if their partner ejaculates, which can be an issue regardless of the genitals. The question goes something like this:

Spit, Swallow, or Let It Wallow?

Spitting the ejaculate out means that as the ejaculation is expelled from the body, the person performing oral sex lets it run out of their mouth. Swallowing means that the person performing oral sex swallows the ejaculate. Letting it wallow means the person performing oral sex holds the ejaculate in their mouth for an extended period of time rather than either spitting or swallowing. Spitting and swallowing are equally fine to do and the choice is only about personal preference. Holding the ejaculate in the mouth, however, increases the potential for STI transmission should the ejaculate be infected, and so it is not recommended.

Anal Sex

Next, we move on to anal sex because anal sex is so often whispered about and then done without important safety precautions. Not to mention the wide range of myths that people believe about it.

Anal sex is stimulation or penetration of the anus by fingers, a penis, or any other object. Here are a few important points about anal sex:

- People of all sexual and gender identities may enjoy anal sex, not just gay men.
- Not all gay men enjoy anal sex.
- You cannot get pregnant from anal sex.
- You can get an STI from anal sex, whether you are penetrating another person or being penetrated.
- Anal sex is unlikely to hurt your sexual health if you take proper precautions.
- Anal sex has the same potential for emotional connection as oral and vaginal sex.

Anal sex needs to be approached thoughtfully, most notably knowing to go slowly and include ample lubricant because the anus is not self-lubricating in the way that the vagina and the mouth are. It is important to use a condom during penetrative anal sex whether the couple is fluid-bonded or not, because of the potential for viruses that are carried through fecal matter. This means that the use of water-based, or condom-friendly, lubricants are really important.

People with prostates, who usually have a penis, may enjoy being penetrated during anal sex because the prostate is connected to the sexual response cycle and the anus is the best way to stimulate the prostate. The other genital anatomy that surrounds the anus is also very sensitive because of the high number of nerve endings going to the area. Therefore, people without a prostate also may enjoy being penetrated during anal sex.

In addition to the physical sensations, people may be aroused by the psychological reaction to engaging in anal sex, which can be seen as pushing against cultural norms. Some people are sexually aroused by doing things that go against cultural acceptance. As long as the sexual activity is physically and emotionally safe, consensual, and ethical, pushing societal boundaries is usually fine. More information about the sexual arousal and response cycle as it applies to less common sexual activities is in Chapter 20.

Vaginal Sex

And here we are at the single act that most people think of as "sex." Although vaginal sex does not necessarily mean penis-in-vagina, that remains what most people think of when they hear the words sex, vaginal sex, intercourse, and vaginal intercourse. In the same way that anal sex can involve being penetrated by a number of different objects, so can vaginal sex. For example, couples without a penis can still engage in vaginal penetration. Fingers and sex toys are the most common non-penile vaginal penetration objects.

The vaginal canal has relatively few nerve endings, particularly when compared to the clitoris or the penis. You may remember that most sexual pleasure from vaginal penetration is actually stimulation of the internal clitoris rather than nerve endings in the vagina itself. Thus, while vaginal sex is often, although not always, pleasurable to the person whose vagina is being penetrated, it is rarely a sexual act that can or should stand alone as the exclusive sexual act a couple engages in. It is important to include other sexual acts, like oral sex or touching the clitoris with fingers, depending on what you and/or your partner find sexually arousing.

A few things to remember about vaginal intercourse:

• While the vagina is self-lubricating, it is common for additional lubricants to be useful and to improve the sexual experience.

- Whenever lubricants are included, it is important to consider the condom-friendliness of them. Water- and silicone-based lubricants are always important when using a condom.

Vaginal sex shouldn't be painful—not even the first time! Return to Chapter 15 for a refresher on how and why.

When Penetration Isn't All That

A couple doesn't have to have oral, anal, or vaginal penetration to have a fulfilling sex life. In fact, when a couple's sexual activities include a wide range of pleasurable activities beyond sex, their experiences are usually better and more frequent. More about foreplay is in Chapter 18. The reason that there may be an increase in frequency of sexual activity if penetrative sex is not the main affair is that penetration can be an emotionally and physically taxing process for the person being penetrated. It physically opens the person being penetrated in a specific and sometimes emotionally draining way. For example, because of the proximity of the digestive tract and the uterus to the vagina and the anus, if someone is feeling sick or pain in those areas, penetration can also hurt. When sex always involves those body parts, many people find it easier to just say no to sex altogether rather than to negotiate a sexual experience that does not include penetration. This is to say nothing of when the vagina, vulva, or anus itself is feeling sensitive. This is why it is useful for couples to expand their sexual activities so that they don't rely on only two or three body parts to feel physically and sexually connected with each other.

Additional Resources

Getting direct, useful information about oral, anal, or vaginal sex that is designed specifically for teenagers and young adults is difficult. Given our culture's preference to keep information about sex from teenagers in the hope that it will prevent them from having sex, there's just very little out there. That said, the best place to get that information, designed for teenagers and young adults, is http://www.Scarleteen.com. At Scarleteen, you'll find real answers, moderated discussion boards, and concrete support.

Before you read this chapter, spend a few minutes reflecting on your thoughts and feelings about these topics and where you've learned what you know about them.

Personal History Q's

1. What does the media tell you about sexual fantasies, pornography, and kink?

2. What have your parents and other influential adults in your life told you about sexual fantasies, pornography, and kink?

3. What do your friends think about sexual fantasies, pornography, and kink?

4. What else do you know about sexual fantasies, pornography, and kink? Where did you learn that information?

5. How much of the information that you've received from all of these different sources do you agree with? Why do you or don't you agree with it?

As you read through the rest of this chapter, remember that what is most important is finding what is right for *you* rather than what is right for someone else.

Some Big Language Ideas

Let's begin by revisiting the words *abnormal, inappropriate,* and *wrong* because those words and ideas are often used about the topics in this chapter. When someone says that a sexual act or feeling is abnormal, inappropriate, or wrong, they are passing judgment on the act or the feeling. The judgment may be moral, religious, based in people's rights, or many other possible factors. Sometimes it boils down to, "That's something I don't want to do." Rather than just saying that they are uninterested in doing something themselves, they also want to stop other people from doing or feeling it. When you're thinking about sexual activities and their moral appropriateness, it is important to sort the conversation into two categories:

1. Things that aren't right for you.

2. Things that aren't right for anyone.

These are really different ideas!

You may well read about sexual activities in this book that feel alien, strange, and unappealing to you personally. And there's nothing wrong with that. As I've said, it's good to have a sense of what feels good to you and your partner and what doesn't. You should never feel pressured to do a sexual act that you're not comfortable with. It doesn't make you a prude or frigid or any of the other negative and degrading words that people use to describe people who are uninterested in sex generally or in specific sexual acts. You don't have to justify why you are interested or uninterested in any sexual activity.

The other category is more problematic. There are some sexual activities that are morally and ethically wrong for everyone. These are activities that invade another person's rights to their own bodily autonomy, like sexual assault and rape. However, it is common for other sexual activities to be judged as wrong for everyone without much reasoning behind that judgment. If someone is old enough to make their own decisions about their sexual autonomy and they are not harming another person, why might their sexual activity or activities be judged by a third person as wrong? What someone often means when they say this is that the activity is wrong for them—but no one is trying to make them do it!

People's judgment of others' sexual activities and their appropriateness can sometimes be influenced by whether the activity is perceived as gross. True, there are probably sexual activities that you would consider to be gross because they squick you out in a real, physical way. You may even be confused by why anyone might consider them sexually appealing. In the times when you react to something as gross, it is important to check yourself for bias. Are you really feeling that the activity or attraction or arousal is gross or wrong for everyone or that it isn't right for you personally? Or do you have some overriding reason why, if done safely and consensually, it should never be done by anyone? These are so different! Know the difference.

Also relevant is the idea of *normal*. What are you really asking when you ask if something, from a specific sexual act to how often someone masturbates, is normal? The word normal is very unspecific. Here are a few of the more specific definitions of *normal*:

1. A sexual activity that most people enjoy.

2. An activity that the majority of popular culture considers to be a common expression of the human sexual experience.

3. A sexual activity that a therapist or a psychiatrist would say is psychologically or emotionally healthy.

Let's think about whether being gay is *normal* according to those three questions. Less than 50% of people identify as gay, but the majority of the US popular culture and therapists agree that it's normal. However, fifty years ago, US popular culture and therapists agreed that identifying as gay was not normal. In those fifty years, there has been a lot of research that has changed people's minds about whether being gay is normal or not. With increased information has come increased understanding about the range of sexual identities that exist and so people see them as normal. Another example might be enjoying masturbation. It is something that more than 80% of all people have done, popular culture is confused about whether it's okay or not, and therapists agree that it's normal and healthy. However, one hundred years ago, the same percentage of people were probably masturbating, but popular culture thought it was very dangerous and therapists were more likely to say that it was not normal. Information, again, is why there was a shift in the popular culture and therapists' understandings. What about things that we currently consider to be abnormal now? Might we consider them normal at some point in the future?

Big Idea Q's

1. Why does it bother someone if another person enjoys a sexual activity that they do not personally enjoy?

2. What are sexual activities that you are not personally interested in?

3. How would you feel if your partner tried to talk you into a sexual activity that you are not interested in?

4. How would you feel if you found out that a friend enjoyed the sexual activity that you do not enjoy and your partner was trying to talk you into doing?

Let's also talk about *too much* sex and sex *addiction*. Sexual activities become a problem when they interfere with the non-sexual aspects of a person's life. Anything from masturbation to watching pornography to sex with a partner can interfere when they become the sole activity a person is interested in. When a person isn't going to school or work, isn't spending time with friends or family, or isn't pursuing their hobbies and interests because of sex, that's a problem. Some people have a hard time reducing the amount of sex they have and they need help to rebalance their lives to be well rounded.

The question of whether sex is truly addictive or not is controversial. Some people say yes, because it can take over people's lives so that they aren't doing anything else. Some people say no, because the brain doesn't have the same kind of chemical process with sex as it does with addictive drugs and alcohol. A biological understanding of addition would say that sex is not addictive. But saying that it is not technically addictive doesn't offer any help when a person feels unable to control how much sex they are having, whether that sex is alone, with pornography, or with one or more partners. There are regrettably few programs that support young women who feel like their consensual sexual behavior is out of their control.

The best place to look for help is probably with a therapist in your area that is sex positive. The American Association of Sexuality Educators, Counselors, and Therapists (http://www.AASECT.org) is the best place to find someone to help you work through any issues you're experiencing. However, just because you find a therapist there, doesn't mean that you're going to click with them. Be willing to look around for someone you click with before you settle. If therapy is too expensive or there's not someone who's an AASECT certified therapist in your area, you may need to make do with someone who is accessible. Many communities have organizations that provide sliding scale therapy. You might try calling your local Planned Parenthood to ask if they have suggestions. Know that you are not alone. Asking for help is not shameful. In fact, it shows how strong you are because you are acknowledging that there is a problem and taking steps to make things better.

Fantasies

Sexual fantasies are an integral part of most people's sexualities. The content or topics of fantasies range dramatically. They can be about certain sexual situations, having sex with certain people, particular sexual acts, or a wide range of other possibilities. What defines a sexual fantasy is the arousal that comes from thinking or daydreaming about the fantasy. Sometimes fantasies are possible, and sometimes fantasies involve people or situations that are not possible. Fantasies may change and evolve as a person gets older and more experienced, or fantasies may stay the same throughout a person's entire life. When fantasies change, they usually do so entirely on their own. It's uncommon for a person to be able to intentionally change their fantasies.

Lots of people worry about their sexual fantasies. If you experience a rich sexual fantasy life, you may question whether your fantasies are normal or safe. If you do not have any sexual fantasies, you may wonder why and worry about whether you are somehow doing it wrong. The reality is, whatever your fantasy life is, it's just fine and you're not doing anything wrong.

Sexual fantasies are not, in and of themselves, wrong. Some sexual fantasies should not be lived out in real life because they would be harmful to the person having them or another person. Being harmful to a partner doesn't include something like consensual spanking during sex, which some people fantasize about and then worry about. When spanking and other activities that include some force are part of healthy, adult, consensual relationships, they can be part of the sexual health of the relationship. It can be emotionally difficult for a caring person to have a sexual fantasy that would create harm were it actually experienced. People with this experience need to get support to manage their desires and sexuality so that they don't actually harm anyone. As when someone feels that they can't control their sexuality, finding a sex-positive therapist through AASECT or another sex-positive organization is very important for guidance and support.

Some people have fantasies that they don't want to experience in real life. This is actually very common for all kinds of fantasies. Just because something sounds like fun when it's imaginary doesn't mean it's going to be fun in reality. Some fantasies can't be lived because of the mythical or imaginary details included, like having a partner who is the size of a giant or having sex with a wizard. These fantasies have to live in the realm of imagination, stories, and maybe through role-play with a partner.

If someone has a healthy and possible sexual fantasy that they do want to experience, it is usually possible to find someone else who has the same, or a similar, fantasy. It may take time to find the right person and it might not be something that becomes a reality until they are over 18 for safety reasons, but it's not something to give up on.

Hiding a sexual fantasy from a partner doesn't usually work in the long run. That doesn't mean that someone should disclose a sexual

- Pornography offers some information about the mechanics of sex in a culture that offers few opportunities for young people looking for information.

- Freedom of speech is one of the most important parts of the United States Bill of Rights, so telling people that they can't create pornography because we don't think it is morally or ethically acceptable is against the very basis of our country's founding.

Research on pornography and its potential positive and negative influences on individuals and the culture at large is incredibly hard to figure out. Most people's opinions about pornography are formed through personal experience and gut emotion rather than through any kind of systematic research. It's unfortunate that we know relatively little about pornography and its effect on people.

What we do know about pornography is that some people don't like it at all and other people like it a lot. We also know that some people feel out of control when it comes to pornography viewing, while others feel in control. We don't know why these differences happen or how to fix the problem for people who feel out of control about pornography. Your personal perspective on pornography is valid, whatever it is.

Pornography Q's

1. Do you have any interest in watching pornography?

2. How would you feel if your partner wanted to watch pornography?

Erotica is a topic usually discussed alongside pornography. The difference between porn and erotica is that pornography is designed be sexually exciting without paying attention to whether it is beautiful or artistic, while erotica is designed to be artistic and the sexually arous-ing aspect of it is secondary. Erotica can refer to stories as well as pic-tures, sculptures, movies, and more.

The most well-known piece of erotica, as of this writing, is the *Fifty Shades* trilogy, beginning with the book *Fifty Shades of Grey.* This originated as a book series and was quickly turned into movies. Let's get this out of the way: *Fifty Shades of Grey* is not an accurate depiction of most BDSM relationships, and if it were telling a true story, it wouldn't be of a healthy relationship. The problem with the primary relationship portrayed in *Fifty Shades of Grey* is that it in-cludes wildly inappropriate usages of power in a relationship as a method of coercion and control, rather than as something to do for fun and emotional and physical sexual fulfillment. It is a description of an abusive BDSM relationship, rather than a healthy BDSM rela-tionship. For many people, *Fifty Shades of Grey* is their only expe-rience with what a relationship that includes BDSM might look like. If you have read the books or watched the movies and feel like you might want to be in a relationship like the one described there, read up on why this story is problematic[1].

If you are over 18 and are interested in reading other, healthy erotica, your local sex toy store will likely have a few suggestions based on your interests.

Sex Toys

Sex toys can include a wide range of things; the most common are vi-brators and dildos. Vibrators vibrate quickly, can be battery charged or can plug into a wall outlet, and are usually used to stimulate the clitoris. Dildos are not powered, come in a variety of sizes and contours, and are usually used to penetrate the vagina or the anus.

If you want to use sex toys by yourself or with a partner, it is very important to use something that is designed for sexual use rather than something you find around the house. It is also important that you buy

---

[1]Here is a good place to start: http://www.theatlantic.com/entertainment/archive/2015/02/consent-isnt-enough-in-fifty-shades-of-grey/385267/

Chapter 21

Books vs. Real Life

This book has incorporated as much real life as possible, through diary entries and invitations for you to think about the content as it applies to you personally, but there is still a gap. For example, the difference between reading and thinking about condoms and actually using a condom is dramatic. This chapter talks about that gap and provides suggestions and support for bridging it.

When You Want to Make It Into Real Life

There are times we read, watch, or learn information about sexuality that we want to carry into real life. This book, for example, provides many things that can support your real-life relationships. You may also have had classes where you have learned useful information or watched movies where you think someone reacted to a situation or hardship with a lot of grace. Bringing information and skills like these into real life takes thought and dedication. Practicing a new skill you hope to develop with a friend, family member, or teacher can help you take that first step.

In the classes I teach about sexuality, I usually set aside an hour or two for communication skills. The time we spend on communication skills is always about how to ask for consent. Middle school students ask each other out on dates. High school students ask about a specific sexual activity that they decide on as a group, which has ranged from holding hands to anal sex. College students think up the hardest, most emotionally difficult relationship-based questions, ranging from "Does this dress make me look fat?" to "Do you love me?" to "I'm pregnant. Do you think I should get an abortion?" Hardly easy questions or conversations to have! After talking about how to ask those questions, we talk about how to answer them. Everyone practices answering the easy way ("No, the dress doesn't make you look fat," "Yes, I love you," although there's not an easy answer about abortion) *and* the hard way ("The dress doesn't flatter your body well," "I care for you, I do not love you," and again, abortion is usually hard to talk about). What this activity does is prepare everyone for thinking about how to ask and answer really hard questions kindly, which should be a goal we aspire to in all of our relationships.

We often use role-play in class to answer questions. Exceptionally romantic declarations of love between two strangers can be both endearing and hilarious, but they aren't real. After everyone role-plays their assigned situation, we talk about what had happened. The people involved in a role-play conversation didn't actually have any real, in-depth connection with each other, and they didn't have any emotional stake in the conversation. If everything went badly, no one was actually hurt. But even in this kind of environment, young women still hesitated to tell someone that they didn't want to go on a date, that they didn't want to have sex, or that they had an abortion. Many young women are hesitant to say things they are worried will hurt someone else, even when they know they won't get hurt and it's just a school assignment.

Hesitation Q's

1. What kinds of things do you hesitate to tell your friends, family, and people you are dating or want to date?

2. Were there any Q's in this book that you hesitated to answer? Why do you think you hesitated, even just for yourself?

3. What could be a good thing about hesitating to answer a question?

4. What could be a bad thing about hesitating to answer a question?

Reading a book and "getting it" doesn't translate directly to being able to put the same ideas into action IRL, even with practice. Why do people who know all about condoms and other kinds of contraception still have high-risk sex? Why do people who are otherwise kind, compassionate human beings ghost instead of honestly turning someone down? Why do people put personal information on the Internet without concern about potential negative impacts?

It's because learning about something you know would be good for you to do in your relationships is very different from doing it in real life. When you're doing something in theory, it's so much easier to know what's right and what's wrong. You can take your time to consider. You can make the decisions without being worried about hurting a real person. You don't have to be worried about your own emotions, either. Real life, of course, isn't like that at all. In real life there are people whose emotions are very real and very raw. In real life there are parents, children, churches, teachers, partners, friends, and doctors who may all have opinions about what you do and why. You can't walk away from real life and the consequences of the choices you make. Because real life is where you have to actually make the decisions and interact with people.

As you move forward in life with the things you've read about and thought about after reading this book, consider what it means to do in real life what you know is the right thing to do. It sometimes helps to think about what someone "should" do in a situation rather than what you actually want to do. Trust that the answers you come to in theory are often the right ones for you to make IRL. Trust in your own ability to do what you know is the right thing to do. You can do it! I know you can.

When You Don't Want to Make It Into Real Life

Taking the good, beautiful things from books, movies, classes, music, and more and bringing them into your real life can be really hard. But most media outlets portray sexual and romantic problems, from lying to a partner to having less-safe sex, and it seems that the negative stories are far more likely to end up being replicated in real life.

Chapter 22

Sexuality Is a Lifelong Thing

Some people feel, at some point in their lives, that they have come to a place of full understanding of their sexual and romantic identities. However, more often people find that sexual and romantic development, learning, and surprises are themes that arise over and over again in their lives. There are many questions and invitations for the reader to engage in sexual and romantic introspection in this book. I hope that you will come back to those questions in the future and see beauty in the process of growing and evolving.

Here you are, at the last chapter of this book. I wonder, as the author of these carefully crafted hundreds of pages of information, whether you have come to this chapter after reading everything that came before, whether you came here first, whether you got bored, or whether you had a question and came here mid-read. I do think this chapter is particularly interesting and is worthy of reading first if you are so inclined.

Here, I offer you an expansive and evolving perspective of sexuality. I hope you come away from these last few pages with a feeling of being in the middle of your own sexual story, with many inopportune, surprising, gentle, pleasurable, and eye-opening moments still to come.

Sexuality evolves along with a person. When I was 13, I worried that I would still be attracted to 13-year-olds when I was 30. But I had no reason to worry because my sexual attractions aged along with me. Sexuality evolves, grows, shifts, and takes on different expressions and desires throughout life. Dig in and enjoy your current sexual feelings and expression and know that they might change as you age. In fact, they probably will.

I just got home from seeing B. It's been a while since I saw him and we spent a couple of hours together, just chilling out and watching TV with our favorite buffalo chicken pizza and wine. And of course we had sex! It was as freaking awesome as usual and it got me thinking how much I've changed since I had my first sexual experiences a few years ago. A that time, it was my first relationship, and while it was great getting to experience sex in all it's glory for the first time with another person, I'm so glad that I am where I am right now. Not just with sex, but with my life — my goals, my career, my body, and I feel like I've finally come to know the real me. Before, I always felt like I gave so much of myself to relationships that I almost forgot who I was — as someone who tends to naturally be kind of nurturing I gave my all to relationships, even if I didn't get anything in return. And it left me empty and heartbroken.

ANJALI

When I decided to go on that pizza date with B, to let things go forward with us, I had gone through so much soul-searching and so much heartbreak that I decided that this time, I wouldn't let myself go when I was with someone else. And honestly, I think it makes my relationship with B so much better. Of course, it's not that I'm in a half-hearted relationship or that I don't care about him — quite the opposite in fact. But this time, I know what I want and I'm not afraid to speak up for myself. My sexuality, my time, my wants and my needs, are all out there and for me at point in my life is take it or leave it. And I love that I can be totally open about it to B, and he's open about what he wants and needs, too. So, we make quite a good team :)

And I'm sure that over the years, whether this relationship stays or goes, I'll be as open as I am with my future partners as I am with B, because I finally feel like me and it's really the BEST feeling in the world!

I am not suggesting that you will necessarily gain knowledge or become better at sexuality just through the process of getting older. Nor am I suggesting that this evolution is a choice you could make in any kind of conscious, planned way, because changing your own sexual desires is not possible. Rather, I am pointing out that what people want, need, and desire evolves over time. Sometimes this evolution does come from learning about yourself and your sexuality, sometimes life circumstances change, and sometimes you yourself change.

While not something to stress out about, it is useful to be open to the future, come what may. The potential of life-long learning about sexuality is best understood through real people's actual lived experiences. To that end, I asked many people the following questions:

What is the most important thing you have learned about your own sexuality? How old were you when you learned it? How old are you now?

The responses I gathered range from the straightforward to the sublime. The authors include people from many walks of life and a wide range of ages. I hope that you'll consider not just the learning that each person experienced, but also what that person might have felt about the matter before they learned what they did about themselves and their sexuality.[1]

> The most important things I've learned are that my sexuality is and always will be an integral part of me, that sexuality is more than having sex, and that my sexuality is good! I learned these truths over time, although I was very fortunate to have wonderful parents who encouraged the growth of my self-concept and self-worth. I'd say I began an awareness of my sexuality around age 12, but certainly I've grown over the years.
> — Dr. Mary Jo, 66

---

[1] Comments provided here were collected and published with permission in response to a Facebook survey I created. Respondents were asked if they wanted to be called by their names or remain anonymous, and I have respected those wishes.

That everything about my sexuality—my body and how it functions, my desires, my identities—is perfectly normal. It was a process, and that process was probably complete by about age 22.

— Jill, 30

That I could bring myself my own sexual pleasure; it was incredibly empowering and encompassed the learning that sexuality is about sharing pleasure (not always a relationship). I was sixteen years old, three years after becoming sexually active.

— Anonymous, 58

I'm demisexual. I first heard the word a year or two ago.

— Dana, 28

The most important thing(s) I learned were about how varied, integral, and all-encompassing sexuality is—from birth to death. I learned that sexuality is so much more than sex, and that it is everything. I was at a week-long sex education retreat and 36 years old.

— Raven Badger, 53

I was an adult when I realized I was gay. I felt stupid for having walked around for so many years with no idea. Was I gay before or did I change? I can't say.

— Anonymous, 39

The most important thing would be that no two people's sexualities are alike, so I don't need to attach myself to another person's definition of who I can like/be attracted to. And that everybody's way of expressing (or not expressing) their sexuality is different. I am pansexual, always knew it but officially affirmed it at 17.

— Isabel, 22

It's not the A + B = C destination-oriented trip I was taught to expect, but rather an ever-unfolding journey that has been lifelong to this point and shows no signs of slowing down. I caught unfocused glimpses of that "journey" message probably in my early 20s, but it didn't really begin to come into clear focus until my late 20s/early 30s. I'm still working

perverted, then they really are what you think (because sex is personal and one's beliefs are so relative). So trust your instinct and run! They're not your right partner, but they may be someone else's. Sex and lovemaking are a deep wide chasm apart. I came to understand that to me, sex is an animal act and serves no purpose in my life. Lovemaking is a spiritual experience that brings transcendence.

— Anonymous, 56

At 22, I learned that I'd been lied to about what sex means to me as a woman. I was free to define that for myself and with my partners.

— Meredith, 39

I learned that bodily fluids are not terrible or gross. I would estimate that I was 30ish when I learned it.

— Adriana, 38

A pivotal moment of sexual learning for me was being a student of Dr. Robert T. Francoeur, an internationally acclaimed sexual scholar as well as a married Catholic priest. Bob taught me that not all Catholics think the same way with respect to sexuality, and he served as a role model, offering new perspectives on Catholicism and sexuality that, until that point, had been only monolithic. I was 23 or 24. I spent three weeks in Denmark with Bob and 17 classmates. Changed my life.

— Bill, 48

It sounds simple, but it was an important lesson for me. I learned that no matter how good or bad I was in bed, how big or small I thought I was perceived as, or how good looking she was, that being "the best I ever had" was about more than just the physical aspect and had a lot to do with how you treated her in the relationship. That gave me the confidence to stop counting orgasms and enjoy the moment as it was intended. I was 26.

— Joseph, 33

I learned more about my sexuality as I grew in my relationships, especially considering I have been in a long-term relationship in most of my adult life. I learned to be more private about my relationships. I learned that not everything is black and white (i.e.: "once a cheater, always a cheater"). I learned that I get to make my own rules in my marriage and I don't have to answer to anyone else. There is no such thing as normal. At age 12, I was taught abstinence-only education, shown scary photos of worst-case scenario STIs, and scared into thinking I would stay a virgin until marriage. This Muslim girl never had the birds and bees talk at home. At age 16, when considering having sex for the first time, I had an upperclassman friend drive me to Planned Parenthood after school so I could talk to someone about safe sex, STI prevention, and how to avoid getting pregnant. I met my now-husband 3 days after turning 20. We got married when I was 23 and he was 25. I truly believe that you can make anything work within a relationship as long as you are committed and openly communicate. I'm still learning.

— Samar, 29

That just because he's my (now ex) boyfriend doesn't mean it's okay for him to have sex with my (drunk) unconscious body. I was 19.

— Angela, 28

I learned in my late teens through my mid-20s that I was turned on by a lot of things and a lot of people, that sexuality was a huge gift and one that delights and inspires me personally and professionally, that your body is amazing and touch is electrifying, more so if you're able to honor the beauty of your body even if it doesn't fit some cultural standard of beauty. Oh, and that orgasms are damn amazing!

— Cat, 41

I'm not sure I can pinpoint a beginning point, but probably starting in my early 30s, I have had a continual learning and growth of the importance and pleasure of presence and connection (energetic, emotional, spiritual) more so than the physical bodily pleasures.

— Bud, 59

That if my heart wasn't in it, my dick usually wasn't either. I was around 23 at the time.

— Andrew, 48

I think one of the toughest things I've done is learn how to accept my sexuality without judging it good or bad. That's been a long, ongoing process, and it's not yet complete—even at 59.

— Paul, 59

Lifelong Learning Q's

1. Which one of the quotes was the most surprising for you? Why?

2. Which one did you relate to the most?

3. What do you hope you will learn about your own sexuality over the next twenty or thirty years?

I hope that these quotes provide you with ample perspectives from which to think about your own process. I hope that if you ever come across a moment where you are hesitant about your next steps in a sexual or romantic relationship, that you will think back to the things these people learned about their sexualities and that they will lend you the strength to dive into the process of expanding your understanding of yourself. There is always room to grow and to learn. Your sexual and romantic life will benefit from it in ways you could never have predicted!

Additional Resources

- "The Questioning Continuum: Seeking Sexuality as a Lifelong Process" on Bitch Media (https://bitchmedia.org/article/questioning-continuum-seeking-sexuality-lifelong-process)

- Sexuality and Aging Today (http://www.sexualityandaging.com/)

Anatomy Glossary

This section is organized in alphabetical order.

Anus: The anus is usually thought of as the part of the body where feces (poop) leave the body, and that is its primary purpose. However, it also has a role in sexual arousal and activity. Some people enjoy anal sex while others don't. Enjoying anal sex is not tied to either sexual orientation or sexual anatomy.

Breasts: Breasts are secondary sex characteristics. Pretty much everyone has breast tissue and nipples, but around puberty, people with a uterus usually develop larger breasts. The size of the breasts is hereditary with some people developing large breasts and other people developing small breasts. The size of the breasts does not impact whether a person is able to breastfeed or not, but it does impact whether the breasts stay higher up or fall lower on the person's body. Whether a person wears a bra or not does not impact this! Most people have one breast that is slightly larger or smaller than the other one.

Cervix: The cervix is the bottom-most part of the uterus. It opens during childbirth. When you hear someone asking how many centimeters dilated a person is during childbirth, they are asking how open the cervix is. The cervix is the part of the anatomy that HPV is the most likely to cause cancerous growths on.

Clitoris: Ahh, the famous clitoris. It's formed from the same embryonic tissue that would have created the penis in a male body, but it has about twice as many nerve endings as a penis. Its job, as far as we know, is solely to bring pleasure. This makes it the only human anatomical body part that we know of that exists only for pleasure, which is just pretty cool. The only part of the clitoris that is external and visible is the glans, which is usually hiding out under the clitoral hood. This hood, which is just a small piece of skin, is located near where the inner labia meet. The majority of the clitoris is internal; it lies inside the body. The internal clitoris is stimulated through the walls of the vagina. When someone with a clitoris is aroused, it usually fills with blood and gets a little bigger.

Epididymis: After sperm is created in the testicles, it moves into the epididymis where it spends two to three months to mature before moving on to the vas deferens.

Fallopian tubes: The fallopian tubes connect the ovaries to the uterus. They help move an egg, or ovum, from the ovary to the uterus. Fertilization of an egg occurs most often in the fallopian tubes.

Foreskin: People with a penis are usually born with a fold of tissue that covers the head of the penis when it is not erect. This tissue is known as the foreskin. In certain places, including the US, it is common for the foreskin to be removed early on in a person's life. A penis with a foreskin is called an intact penis, while a penis where the foreskin has been removed is called a circumcised penis. The act of circumcision is influenced a lot by culture, rather than science.

G-spot (or, Gräfenberg spot): The g-spot refers to a general area in the vaginal canal toward the front and a little ways in. The g-spot can vary in size, with some vaginas having large ones and some having none at all. We don't know a lot about the g-spot, and some people even deny its existence, which is confusing to the people who have one. Some people find having their g-spot touched to be sexually arousing and other people find it uncomfortable. It is likely connected in some way to vaginal ejaculations.

Hymen: The poor hymen. It's just a simple membrane, but it's been subjected to a lot of misinformation for several thousands of years. It is a stretchy membrane designed to protect a fetus's vagina while still in the uterus. After birth it doesn't really have much purpose, and it starts to slowly degrade. The hormones that get puberty started make the hymen break much more easily. By the time someone starts their period, the hymen is usually either entirely gone or is only a small rim inside the vagina. In a few people, the hymen may still cover most of or all of the vaginal opening. In these cases, minor surgery may be performed to create perforations in the hymen so that menstrual fluid can exit. Throughout the course of a child's life, the hymen may be stretched or torn by a variety of different things—including strenuous athletic activity. When the hymen does stretch or tear, it can sometimes bleed a little bit and cause some slight discomfort. Not having a hymen does not mean that someone has had penetrative vaginal sex.

Inner labia: Also known as the labia minora or inner lips, these are folds of skin found right inside the outer labia. Along with the outer labia, they work to help protect the openings of the urethra and the vagina. Some people also have pubic hair on the inner labia.

Mons veneris: This Latin term translates to the "Mount of Venus." Venus was the goddess of love in Roman culture. The mons veneris is the fatty tissue covering the pubic bone. During puberty, pubic hair often grows here.

Outer labia: Also known as the labia majora or outer lips, these are folds of skin that reach from the mons veneris to the perineum. The perineum is the skin between the opening of the vagina and the anus. Pubic hair also often grows on the outer labia.

Ovaries: The ovaries are found at the end of the fallopian tubes. They are pretty talented, as they release hormones into the body and also house the cells that will become ova. These cells are called oocytes. After puberty, one (or sometimes two) oocytes develop into ova every month and then head out into the fallopian tubes.

Penis: The penis has a lot of jobs. It's the site of sexual pleasure and it houses the urethra, where both urine and ejaculate can pass through. The penis is filled with spongy tissue that, when filled with blood, causes the penis to become erect (larger and hard).

Perineum: The perineum is the skin between the opening of the vagina and the anus. A common slang term for this is the *taint*. A silly saying explains this term—it's called the taint because it 'taint the vagina and it 'taint the anus.

Prostate: The prostate works as the joining place for the vas deferens, the seminal vesicles, and the urethra as it exits the bladder. It creates some of the ejaculatory fluid that mixes with the sperm and the fluid from the seminal vesicles. It also prevents urine and ejaculate from coming out of the penis at the same time. Some people find the prostate sexually arousing when stimulated through the anus.

Pubic hair: This is the hair that often appears at puberty and can grow on the mons veneris, labia, and perineum. It can also grow around the penis and the scrotum. In the last several decades, there have been lots of changes in pubic hair grooming trends. Some people may trim, shave, or wax part or all of their pubic hair. This is absolutely a matter of personal choice, though removing pubic hair may cause increases in skin irritation, ingrown hairs, and risk of infection.

Scrotum: The scrotum, also known as the scrotal sack or just "the sack," is where the testicles are held.

Seminal vesicles: The seminal vesicles produce some of the fluid that is ejaculated from the penis.

Smegma: Almost every single person, regardless of anatomy, produces smegma. Smegma is thought to be a mix of dead skin cells and oils that is shed from the genitalia. There's also research suggesting that it's another natural lubricant that our body uses to facilitate sexual activity. Unfortunately, it's gotten a bad reputation. This may be due in part to that fact that, if it is allowed to build up over a period of time, it can become white or yellow and start to smell. It can also cause some irritation if it is allowed to build up, especially under the foreskin. It may also get a bad rap because, honestly, smegma is just a ridiculous sounding word.

Testicles: More commonly known as "balls," the testicles are usually found right below the penis. There are usually two, and it's pretty common for one to hang down slightly below the other. They're a lot like the ovaries in that they release hormones into the body and function as the site of sperm production.

Urethra: Almost everyone, regardless of sex assignment, has a urethra. For individuals with vulvas, the urethral opening is located above the vagina and below the clitoris. The urethra is a tube-shaped structure, and in a person with a vulva, its sole responsibility is to carry urine out from the bladder. The urethra in people with vulvas is about two inches long. For people with penises, the urethral opening is usually found at the head of the penis. It can carry both urine and semen out of the body. In someone with a penis, the urethra is about eight inches long on average.

Uterus: The uterus, also sometimes known as the womb, works to direct blood flow during sexual response and provides a habitat for a fetus to develop. The bottom part of the uterus, known as the cervix, leads out into the vagina. Up top, the uterus usually connects to two fallopian tubes. At the end of the fallopian tubes are the ovaries. After reaching puberty, many people with a uterus will go through the menstrual cycle. Part of this cycle includes prepping the uterus for a possible egg that has been fertilized by a sperm. If a fertilized egg does show up, it usually implants itself into the endometrium, or inner layer of the uterus. This is the beginning of a pregnancy. If an egg is not implanted, the menstrual cycle continues on its merry way and the lining of the endometrium is shed during menstruation, or the period. After this shedding, the uterus starts rebuilding the endometrium and the cycle continues.

Vagina: The vagina is a muscular canal found below the urethra in people with vulvas. It's made up of three main layers—the inner mucosal layer, the middle layer of muscle, and the outer layer of connective tissue. The vagina is a multi-talented structure. It's connected to the uterus, and it provides an exit for menstrual blood for individuals who have periods. Additionally, the vagina plays an important role in pregnancy, as this is where semen is ejaculated and the canal through which a baby is born. We talk more about pregnancy, birth, and the vagina in

Chapter 6. The vagina can also be a source of pleasure during sexual arousal and stimulation. The bottom one-third of the vagina has nerve endings that can be stimulated and provide pleasure. Fingers, mouths, penises, or sex toys can cause this pleasure. When aroused, the vagina often expands in both width and length. It also produces lubrication, which can make penetration of the vagina easier. There's one more important thing that the vagina can do—it can clean itself! The vagina is a self-cleaning organ that is usually capable of maintaining a happy, acidic environment. Certain products are sold to "clean" the vagina, but these can actually disrupt the vagina's environment and leave you prone to infections.

Vas deferens: The vas deferens is the duct that moves the sperm from the epididymis in the scrotum up, over the bladder, and around to the back of the penis where it joins with the fluid from the seminal vesicles and the prostate.

Vulva: Collectively describes the mons veneris, the outer and inner labia, the clitoris, and the openings of the vagina and the urethra. People often say vagina when they mean vulva.

Bibliography

Chapter 1: Who Are You?

boyd, d. (2014). It's complicated: The social lives of networked teens. New Haven, MA: Yale University Press.

Davis, K. (2013). Young people's digital lives: The impact of interpersonal relationships and digital media use on adolescents' sense of identity. *Computers in Human Behavior, 29*(6), 2281–2293.

Chapter 2: Gender and Identity

Dreger, A. (2015). *Galileo's middle finger: Heretics, activists, and the search for justice in science.* New York, NY: Penguin Press.

Ryan, C. & Jethá, C. (2010). *Sex at Dawn: The prehistoric origins of modern sexuality.* New York, NY: HarperCollins.

Chapter 3: Attraction

Blank, H. (2012). *Straight: The surprisingly short history of heterosexuality.* Boston, MA: Beacon Press.

Laughlin, S. (2016, March 11). Gen Z goes beyond gender binaries in new Innovation Group data [Blog post]. Retrieved from https://www.jwtintelligence.com/2016/03/gen-z-goes-beyond-gender-binaries-in-new-innovation-group-data/

Chapter 4: Inside and Outside Bodies

Corinna, H. (2012, November 27). Honorably discharged: A guide to vaginal secretions [Blog post]. Retrieved from http://www.scarleteen.com/article/bodies/honorably_discharged_a_guide_to_vaginal_secretions

Corinna, H. (2016, May 26). On the rag: A guide to menstruation [Blog post]. Retrieved from http://www.scarleteen.com/article/bodies/on_the_rag_a_guide_to_menstruation

Corinna, H. (2016, May 31). With pleasure: A whole view of sexual anatomy for every body [Blog post]. Retrieved from http://www.scarleteen.com/article/bodies/with_pleasure_a_view_of_whole_sexual_anatomy_for_every_body

Fayed, L. (2016, April 7). Adding vulvar self-exam to your at-home routine [Blog post]. Retrieved from https://www.verywell.com/vulvar-self-exam-514538

Intersex Society of North America: http://www.isna.org/

King, B. M. (2012). *Human sexuality today.* Upper Saddle River, NJ: Pearson Education.

Lopez, K. & Jones, R. (2014). *Human reproductive biology* (4th ed.). San Diego, CA: Academic Press.

U.S. Department of Health and Human Services, Office of Disease Prevention and Health Promotion. (2016, August 26). Get your well-woman visit every year. Retrieved from https://healthfinder.gov/HealthTopics/Category/everyday-healthy-living/sexual-health/get-your-well-woman-visit-every-year

Chapter 5: STIs and Prevention

Grimes, J. (2016). *Seductive delusions: How everyday people catch STIs.* Baltimore, MD: Johns Hopkins University Press.

Sweeney, M. M. & Grisman, R. K. (2005). *Condom sense: A guide to sexual survival in the new millennium*. New York, NY: Lantern Books.

Chapter 6: Pregnancy and Prevention

Cassel, C. (2015). *Why knocked up?: The paradox of sex, magical thinking, and accidental pregnancy in this age of contraception*. Xlibris.

Jerman, J., Jones, R. K., & Onda, T. (2016). *Characteristics of U.S. abortion patients in 2014 and changes since 2008*. New York, NY: Guttmacher Institute.

Lopez, K. & Jones, R. (2014). *Human reproductive biology* (4th ed.). San Diego, CA: Academic Press.

Roach, M. (2009). *Bonk: The curious coupling of science and sex*. New York, NY: W.W. Norton & Company.

Sanger, A. (2004). *Beyond choice: Reproductive freedom in the 21st century*. New York, NY: PublicAffairs.

Chapter 7: Decision Making

Bromberg, U., Wiehler, A., & Peters, J. (2015). Episodic future thinking is related to impulsive decision making in healthy adolescents. *Child Development, 86*(5), 1458–1468.

Hensel, D.J., Hummer, T. A., Acrurio, L. R., James, T. W., & Fortenberry, J. D. (2015). Feasibility of functional neuroimaging to understand adolescent women's sexual decision making. *Journal of Adolescent Health, 56*(4), 389–395.

Chapter 8: Communication

Widman, W., Nesi, J., Choukas-Bradley, S, & Prinstein, M. (2014). Safe sext: Adolescents' use of technology to communicate about sexual health with dating partners. *Journal of Adolescent Health, 54*(5), 612–614.

Chapter 9: Healthy Relationships 101

Halpern-Meekin, S., Manning, W. D., Giordano, P. C., & Longmore, M. A. (2013). Relationship churning, physical violence, and verbal abuse in young adult relationships. *Journal of Marriage and Family, 75*(1), 2–12.

Chapter 10: Hooking Up

Garcia, J. R., Reiber, C., Massey, S. G., & Merriwether, A. M. (2012). Sexual hookup culture: A review. *Review of General Psychology, 16*(2), 161–176.

Chapter 12: Being in a Relationship

Collins, W. A., & van Dulmen, M. (2016). "The Course of True Love(s)..." Origins and pathways in the development of romantic relationships. In Booth, A, Crouter, A. C., & Snyder, A. (Eds.), *Romance and sex in adolescence and emerging adulthood: Risks and opportunities* (pp. 63–86). New York, NY: Routledge.

Chapter 14: Consent, Harassment, Sexual Assault, and Rape

Rape, Abuse & Incest National Network. (n. d). *The criminal justice system: Statistics*. Retrieved from https://www.rainn.org/statistics/criminal-justice-system

Rape, Abuse & Incest National Network. (n. d). *Perpetrators of sexual violence: Statistics*. Retrieved from https://www.rainn.org/statistics/perpetrators-sexual-violence

Sexual harassment. 29 CFR § 1604.11 (2012).

U.S. Department of Education, Office for Civil Rights. (2008). *Sexual harassment: It's not academic.* Retrieved from https://www2.ed.gov/about/offices/list/ocr/docs/ocrshpam.html

U.S. Department of Justice, Office on Violence Against Women. (n. d.). *Sexual assault.* Retrieved from https://www.justice.gov/ovw/sexual-assault

U.S. Department of Justice, Office of Public Affairs. (2012, January 6). An updated definition of rape [Blog post]. Retrieved from https://www.justice.gov/opa/blog/updated-definition-rape

World Association for Sexual Health. (2014). *Declaration of Sexual Rights.* Retrieved from http://www.worldsexology.org/resources/declaration-of-sexual-rights/

Chapter 15: Your First Time

Else-Quest, N. M. (2014). Robust but plastic: Gender differences in emotional responses to sexual debut. *The Journal of Sex Research, 51*(4), 473–476.

Vasilenko, S. A., Maas, M. K., & Lefkowitz, E. S. (2014). "It felt good but weird at the same time": Emerging adults' first experiences of six different sexual behaviors. *Journal of Adolescent Research, 30*(5), 586–606.

Chapter 16: Orgasms

Jones, E. (1953). *Sigmund Freud: Life and work.* New York, NY: Basic.

Solot, D., & Miller, M. (2007). *I <3 female orgasm.* New York, NY: Marlowe & Company.

Chapter 17: Masturbation

Bockting, W. O. (2002). Introduction. *Journal of Psychology and Human Sexuality, 14*(2–3), 1-4.

Pinkerton, S. D., Bogart, L.M., Cecil, H., & Abramson, P. R. (2002). Factors associated with masturbation in a collegiate sample. *Journal of Psychology and Human Sexuality, 14*(2–3), 104.

Chapter 18: Foreplay, Making Out, and Attraction

Kirshenbaum, S. (2011). *The science of kissing: What our lips are telling us.* New York, NY: Hachette Book Group.

Chapter 19: Oral, Anal, and Vaginal Sex

The Guttmacher Institute. (2016, September). *American teens' sexual and reproductive health* [Fact sheet]. Retrieved from https://www.guttmacher.org/fact-sheet/american-teens-sexual-and-reproductive-health

Chapter 20: Fantasy, Kink, and Pornography

Klein, M. (2012). *America's war on sex: The continuing attack on law, lust, and liberty* (2nd ed.). Santa Barbara, CA: Praeger.

Ogas, O., & Gaddam, S. (2012). *A billion wicked thoughts: What the Internet tells us about sexual relationships.* New York, NY: Plume.

Chapter 22: Sexuality Is a Lifelong Thing

Ponzetti, J. J. Jr. (2016). *Evidence-based approaches to sexuality education: A global perspective.* New York, NY: Routledge.

World Health Organization. (2010). Developing sexual health programmes: A framework for action. (WHO Reference No. WHO/RHR/HRP/10.22). Retrieved from http://www.who.int/reproductivehealth/publications/sexual_health/rhr_hrp_10_22/en/

Index

AASECT. *See* American Association of Sexuality Educators, Counselors, and Therapists

"Abnormal" sexual activities, 312–314

Abortions, 112–116

Abstinence, 123, 243

Abusive relationship(s), 163–164

  ending, 209–210

  in *Fifty Shades of Grey*, 323

Addiction

  to porn, 321

  to sex, 315–316

Adoption agencies, 118

Adoptive parents, finding, 118

Ageism, 200

AIDS (acquired immunodeficiency syndrome), 91

Alcohol use, consent and, 224, 226–227, 238

Ally, 49

American Association of Sexuality Educators, Counselors, and Therapists (AASECT), 267, 316, 317

Anal douches, 80–81

Anal sex, 305–306

  hygiene practices for, 80–81

  Lina G.'s diary entry on, 303

Anatomy. *See also* Body

  and body image, 84–86

  female, 70–71

  male, 71–72

  and sex assignment, 67, 68

  sexual, 66–73

  terms related to, 347–352

Androphilic, 49, 61

Anjali, 11

  on communication, 153–155

  on contraception, 124–126, 140–142

  on different view of sex, 308–310

  on evolution of sexuality, 336–337

  on first sexual intercourse, 254–256

  on masturbation, 284–286

  on orgasms, 272–273

  on societal and cultural norms, 37–39

  on STIs, 104–106

Annual physical exams, 83–84

Anus, 70–71, 347

  cleanliness of, 80–81

  penetration of, 245

  using condom when stimulating, 282

Appearance

  and assumed desire for sex, 224

  assumptions based on, 18, 36

  Blake's diary entry on, 27–28

  choices about, 18

  and consent, 238

  as legal issue, 229

  others' treatment based on, 16

Aromantic, 49

Arousal, 76–78

  with fetishes, 319

  as purpose of porn sex, 320

  during rape, 238

  with sexual fantasies, 316

  sexual touching, 298–299

Arousal cycle, 261, 306

Asexual, 49

Asking someone out, 184–187, 191. *See also* Dating

  communication when, 185, 187

  as harassment, 231

Assault. *See* Sexual assault

Assumption(s)

  about gender expression, 35

  about gender roles, 36, 41–42

  about rape, 237–239

  based on appearance, 18, 36

  based on interests, 18–19

  cultural, about orgasm, 265–267

  of heterosexism, 58–61

  that sex comes naturally, 301

Attempted rape. *See* Sexual assault

Attraction, 47–63

  and coming out, 53–57

  and flirting, 292–295

  Genderbread Person, 50–52

  and homophobia and heterosexism, 58–61

  how sexual orientation/identity and gender identity go together, 61–62

  Jordan's diary entry on, 51

  and language of sexual orientation/identity, 47–50

  Margaret's diary entry on, 63

  sexual and romantic, 50–52

Authenticity, 25–26

  online, 22

  in physical appearance, 18

Autonomy, right to, 228

AVERT, 93

Babies, items required for, 116–117
Bacterial STIs, 94–95
Bacterial vaginosis (BV), 79–80
Balance, in relationships, 201–203, 207
Barrier contraceptives, 120–121
BDSM, 319–320, 323
Behavioral contraceptive methods, 123
Being asked out, 188–189
Being in a relationship, 193–204
    avoiding, 197, 203
    decision making about, 203
    and falling in love, 200–201
    finding balance, 201–203
    finding "the one," 201
    handling problems, 198–200
    masturbation while, 287
    private aspects of, 196
    public aspects of, 194–195
    reasons for, 193
Biological sex, 30–34
    benefit of becoming aware of, 34
    body parts related to, 68–73
    Erin's diary entry on, 33
    expressing. See Gender expression
    and gender identity, 34
    and sexual orientation/identity, 61
Biology
    definition of, 30
    of orgasms, 260–262
    of pregnancy, 108, 110–111
    sexual, 65–66. See also Body
Biphobia, 56
Birth control. See also Condoms
    contraception, 120–125
    Margaret's diary entry on, 109
    non-ejaculating orgasms as form of, 269
    and pregnancy prevention, 112
Bisexual, 48, 61
Bladder, 71
Blake, 11
    on appearance, 27–28
    on asking someone out, 191
    on coming out, 54
    on communication, 150–151
    on first sex, 252
    on gender stereotypes, 45–46
    on masturbation, 278–279
    on orgasm, 270
    on sexual assault, 233–234
    on sexual pleasure, 278–279
    on STIs, 92
    on unhealthy relationships, 169–170

Bodily integrity, right to, 228
Body, 65–88
    annual physical exams, 83–84
    arousal and pleasure, 76–78
    biology, 65–66
    body parts related to sex, 68–73
    cleanliness, 78–81
    menstrual cycle, 73–76
    self-exams, 81–83
    and self-love, 84–86
    sex, 67–68
    sexual anatomy, 66–67
    touching parts of, 298–299
Body image, 84–86
Body language, 17–18
Bondage, 319–320, 323
boyd, danah, 22–24
Brain, 72, 78
Brand, 15–21
    authenticity of, 25
    in f2f life, 15–21
    in online life, 21–25
    people's reactions to, 25–26
Breaking up. See Ending relationships
Breast cancer, 82
Breast exam, 83–84
Breasts, 71, 72, 347
Breast self-exams, 82–83
Buck, Pearl S., 332
BV (bacterial vaginosis), 79–80

Cervical cap, 121
Cervix, 70, 347
Cheating, 215–216
Child molestation. See Sexual assault
Chlamydia, 94
Chromosomes, 68–69
Circumcised penis, 70
Cisgender, 34–35
Cleanliness, 78–81
Clitoral hood, 71
Clitoral orgasms, 262, 264
Clitoris, 70, 71, 78, 347–348
    internal, 70, 71, 306
    and masturbation, 280, 282
    in oral sex, 302
    and orgasm, 261–262
    stimulation by vibrators, 323
Clothing, consent and, 238
Coercion, freedom from, 228
Columns and Shadows: A Healthy
    Relationship Model, 158–161
Coming out, 53–57

about gender identity, 35
about sexual orientation, 35
approaches to, 55–56
Blake's diary entry on, 54
Erin's diary entry on, 57, 344
relationships with partners who are not
"out" yet, 166, 167
Communication, 143–155. *See also*
Language
about orgasms, 271
about sexual firsts, 247
about things leading to orgasm, 266
Anjali's diary entry on, 153–155
Blake's diary entry on, 150–151
in branding, 15
bringing up relationship problems, 198,
200
for clear consent, 225–226
developing skills in, 329–330
Erin's diary entry on, 151
in face-to-face vs. in online interactions,
23–24
honesty about yourself in, 143–146
listening, 148–149
Margaret's diary entry on, 147
nonverbal, 17–18
online, 21–24
in private times of relationships, 196
talking, 146–148
when asking someone out, 185, 187
when coming out, 55–56
when you are asked out, 188–189
Community. *See also* Support
for BDSM information and support, 319,
320
in supporting pregnant teenagers, 117
wisdom and insight from, 207–208
Complimenting others, when flirting,
292–293
Condoms, 92
and anal stimulation, 282
as barrier contraceptives, 120–121
external and internal, 120–121
lubricants with, 103
to prevent STIs, 102–103, 105–106
risk with, 247
when masturbating, 282
Consent, 219–229
and alcohol or drug use, 226–227
meaning of, 220–223
no means no rule of, 224, 232
from partners, 251

and rape, 238
and rights of individuals, 228–229
rules of, 224–226
and sexual assault, 232
topics related to, 247
types of, 223–224
withdrawing, 238
yes means yes rule of, 226, 232
Consent: Not Actually That Complicated
(Emmeline May), 219–223
Contraception, 120–123. *See also* Birth
control
Anjali's diary entry on, 124–126
barrier methods of, 120–121
hormonal forms of, 74, 121–122
Cramps, during menstrual cycle, 74–75
Cultural norms
Anjali's diary entry on, 37–39
concerning rape, 236
for dating, 183–184
for families, 40
for relationships, 37–40
Culture(s)
and administration of laws, 229
and gender, 37–40
and gender expression, 31
and gender roles, 41–42
of heterosexism, 58–61
homophobic subcultures, 58
influence of pornography in, 322
and nonverbal communication, 17, 18
and "normal" sexual activities/identities,
314–315
of orgasms, 265–267
and perspectives on fantasy,
pornography, and kink, 311
and punishment for negative sexual
activities, 228
rape, 237–239
that prize virginity, 244, 245

Dangerous thought processes, Jordan's
diary entry on, 186
Dating, 183–191
being asked out, 188–189
breaking up. *See* Ending relationships
in high school, 201
how to ask someone out, 185–187
and New Relationship Energy, 189–190
old-fashioned process of, 183–184
for prom, 187
who asks the other out?, 184–185
Decision making, 129–142

about being in a relationship, 203
about coming out, 53, 55
about ending relationships, 206-208
about hooking up, 174-175
about masturbation, 283
about online activities, 24
about pregnancy, 111-120
about pursuing interests, 19
about sexual firsts, 247-248
Anjali's diary entry on, 140-142
by default, 134-135
Erin's diary entry on, 132
examples of, 133-134
by gut reaction, 135
in real life, 331
sexual, 130-133
by system, 136-138
Default, decisions made by, 134-135
Demisexual, 49
Dental dam, 103
Diaphragm, 121
Dildos, 323
Discipline, 319-320, 323
Disclosure, of sexually transmitted
   infections, 102
Doing the right thing, 332
Dominance, 319-320, 323
Drifting apart, 214-215
Drug use, consent and, 226-227
The Duluth Model (of relationships), 158
Dumping someone, 205

Egg, in menstrual cycle, 73, 74
Ejaculations
   during oral sex, 304-305
   from penis, 268, 269
   for pregnancy, 108
   from vagina, 258, 259, 261-262,
      268-269
Embarrassment, about unhealthy
   relationships, 167-168
Emergency contraception, 121-122
Emojis, 293
Emotional control, in rape, 238
Emotions (feelings)
   about hooking up, 175-176
   expressing, when asking someone out, 185
   following rape or sexual assault, 237
   in long-lasting relationships, 206-207
   in new relationships, 189-190
   with oral sex, 302
   and PMS, 75
   with pregnancy, 107

in real life, 331
in reporting rape/sexual assault, 236,
237
when online, 22
when relationships end, 210-213
when you are asked out, 188
Ending relationships, 205-218
   Erin's diary entry on, 218
   feelings when, 210-212
   healthy relationships, 210
   Jordan's diary entry on, 211
   by just drifting apart, 214-215
   language related to, 205
   making decisions about, 206-208
   and monogamy, 217
   reasons for, 208-209
   unhealthy or abusive relationships, 168,
      209-210
   when other person ends it, 212-213
   when someone cheats, 215-216
Endometriosis, 74-75
Enemas, 80-81
Epididymis, 71, 348
Equality, in relationships, 158-161
Erin
   on coming out, 57, 344
   on communication, 151
   on decision making, 132
   on ending relationships, 218
   on evolution of sexuality, 344
   on gender expression and biological
      sex, 33
   on a healthy relationship, 166
   on masturbation, 288
   on puberty, 87
   on self-love, 87
   on unwanted touching, 240
Erotica, 322-323
Ethical consumption of porn, 321
Ethically wrong sexual activities, 313
Evolution of sexuality, 335-344
   Anjali's diary entry on, 336-337
   Erin's diary entry on, 344
   Jordan's diary entry on, 340
Exhale, 116
Eye contact
   as communication, 17-18
   in flirting, 292

Fabric pads, 76
Face-to-face (f2f) interactions
   in f2f life, 15-21
   identities, 16-17

interests, 18–19
language, 17
nonverbals, 17–18
people you spend time with, 19, 21
physical appearance, 18
Facial expressions, 17–18
Falling in love, 200–201
Fallopian tubes, 74, 348
Family(-ies)
coming out to, 35, 55
cultural norms for, 40
and people's perceptions of who you
are, 19, 21
and perspectives on fantasy,
pornography, and kink, 311
perspectives on gender in, 40–42
Fantasies, 316–318
Fear
of first penetration, 245
of talking about fantasies, 318
Feelings. See Emotions
Female, 67
Female anatomy, 70–71
Female-ness. See Biological sex
Feminine. See Gender expression
Fetish, 318–320
Fifty Shades trilogy, 323
Fingers, 78
Firsts, 243–256
Blake's diary entry on, 252
making decisions about, 247–248
with a new partner, 250–253
oral sex as, 302
and pain of penetration, 244–246
preparing for, 248–250
Flirting, 292–295
and consent, 238
as sexual harassment, 230–231
unconscious, 294
unreciprocated, 293–294
Fluid exchange (STIs), 96, 99, 102–103
"Folding Chair" (Regina Spektor), 84
Fondling. See Sexual assault
Forcible sodomy. See Sexual assault
Foreplay. See Low-risk sexual activities
Foreskin, 70–72, 80, 348
Francoeur, Robert T., 342
Free bleeding, 76
Freedom from violence/coercion, right
to, 228
Freedom of speech, 322
Freud, Sigmund, 264

Friends
advice about sexual firsts from, 248, 251
coming out to, 55
rapes by, 236
Friendships. See also Relationships
drifting apart in, 214
mutual interests in, 19
and people's perceptions of who you
are, 19, 21
Gaslight (play), 164
Gaslighting, 164–165
Gay
definition of, 48
as normal, 314
Gender, 29–46
assumptions in same-gender
relationships, 42–43
and culture, 37–40
definition of, 29
family's perspectives on, 40–42
and identity, 29–35
language related to, 29–30, 34
rape and, 238
and relationships, 36
Genderbread Person, 30, 31, 50–52
Gender expression, 31
changes in, 35
definition of, 30
Erin's diary entry on, 33
and sexual orientation/identity, 61
sexual orientation vs., 35
Gender identity, 31
benefit of becoming aware of, 34
and biological sex, 34
changes in, 35
coming out about, 35
definition of, 30
language involving, 61
and sexual orientation/identity, 61–62
Gender nonconforming, 34
Gender norms, Anjali's diary entry on,
37–39
Genderqueer, 34
Gender roles, 36, 43–44
assumptions about, 36, 41–42
in dating, 184–185
in same-gender relationships, 42–43
Gender stereotypes, 36
Blake's diary entry on, 45–46
in same-gender relationships, 42–43
Genitalia, 69–72
changes in, 81

in oral sex, 302, 304
and orgasms, 258, 261–262
pleasure from, 78
self-exams of, 81–82
Glans, 72, 78
Go Ask Alice, 280
Golden Rule, 203
Gonorrhea, 94
G-spot (Gräfenberg spot), 70, 268, 348
Gut reaction, decisions made by, 135
Guttmacher Institute, 116, 280
Gynephilic, 49, 61
Health
    and masturbation, 282
    right to, 229
Healthy relationships, 157–170
    Columns and Shadows model of, 158–161
    ending, 208, 210
    Erin's diary entry on, 166
    hookups, 177–178
    and signs of unhealthy relationships, 161–168
Hepatitis B, 90
Herpes simplex virus (HSV), 90–91, 104–106
Heterosexism, 58–61
Heterosexual, 48
HIV (human immunodeficiency virus), 91, 93
Homophobia, 56, 58–61
Honesty
    about yourself in communication, 143–146
    when asking someone out, 187
    when hooking up, 173–174
    when you are asked out, 188
Hooking up, 171–182
    act of, 174–175
    choosing partner for, 177–178
    definition of, 174
    language of, 171–174
    Lina G.'s diary entry on, 181–182
    making decisions about, 174–175
    motivations for, 178–179
    risks involved in, 171–172, 175–177
    sexual activities involved in, 171–172, 174
    understanding your feelings about, 175–176
Hormonal contraception, 74, 121–122
Hormones, 72
HPV (human papillomavirus), 93–94
HSV (herpes simplex virus), 90–91, 104–106
Human immunodeficiency virus (HIV), 91, 93
Human papillomavirus (HPV), 93–94
Hymen, 244–245, 348–349
Identity(-ies). See also Presenting yourself
    in f2f interactions, 16–17
    gender, 61–62
    gender and, 29–35
    and interests, 18–19
    people's reactions to, 26
    and people you spend time with, 19, 21
    and physical appearance, 18
    sexual. See Sexual orientation/identity
    visible and invisible, 16
Illegal sexual activities. See Negative sexual activities
Implant contraceptive, 121
Inappropriate sexual activities, 312–314
Incest. See Sexual assault
Incubation period (STIs), 96, 99
Infections, of vagina, 79–80
Inner labia, 70, 71, 349
In-person interactions. See Face-to-face (f2f) interactions
Intent, in unhealthy relationships, 165–166
Interests, 18–19
Internal clitoris, 70, 71, 306
Intersex, 67–69
    definition of, 49
    and masturbation, 282
Intimacy, 196. See also Sexual activities; specific practices or topics
    advice on, 297–298
    and hooking up, 172, 178
    of oral sex, 302
    private moments of, 196
Intrauterine device (IUD), 121
It's Complicated (danah boyd), 24
Jane's Due Process, 116
Jordan, 11–12
    on advice, 333
    on an unhealthy relationship, 162
    on breaking up, 211
    on dangerous thought processes, 186
    on evolution of sexuality, 340
    on kink, 325
    on kissing, 300
    on masturbation, 281
    on orgasms, 259
    on procrastination, 333
    on scars, 325

on sexual/romantic orientation, 51
on social media, 20
Justice, right to, 229
Kink, 318–320
    definition of, 49, 319
    Jordan's diary entry on, 325
Kirshenbaum, Sheril, 298
Kissing, 296–298
    and consent, 238
    first time for, 246, 247
    Jordan's diary entry on, 300
Klinefelter syndrome, 69
Labia
    inner, 70, 71, 349
    in masturbation, 280, 282
    in oral sex, 302, 304
    outer, 70, 71, 349
Language. *See also* Communication
    appropriate and inappropriate, 17
    around abstinence, 243
    around explicit consent, 232
    around orgasms, 257
    around sex, 9
    around sexuality/sexual acts, 9, 312–316
    around virginity, 243
    of ending relationships, 205
    in f2f interactions, 17
    of hooking up, 171–174
    involving gender identity, 61
    nonverbal, 17–18
    related to gender, 29–30, 34
    of sexual orientation/identity, 47–50
    of STIs and STDs, 89–90, 96
    when coming out, 55–56
Legal issues
    concerning negative sexual activities,
    228. *See also* Negative sexual activities
    cultural influence in, 229
Lesbian(s)
    definition of, 48
    gender assumptions by, 42–43
LGBTQ+, 48
Lice, pubic, 95
Lina G., 12
    on anal sex, 303
    on being pregnant, 114
    on homophobia, 60
    on hookups, 181–182
    on losing virginity, 249
    on masturbation, 289
    on oral sex, 303
    on orgasms, 263

on problems in a relationship, 202
    on self-love, 85
    on STIs, 97–98
Linney, Laura, 332
Lips, 78
Listening, 148–149
Logistics of relationships, 203
Long-term relationships, 203, 206–207
Love
    finding "the one," 201
    and healthy relationships, 201
    public vs. private declaration of, 203
    self-, 84–87
    teenagers falling in, 200–201
LoveisRespect.org, 165, 168
Low-risk sexual activities, 291–300
    flirting, 292–295
    kissing, 296–298
    touching sexually, 298–299
Lubricants
    for anal sex, 305
    with condoms, 103
    for oral sex, 304
    for painful penetration, 246
    for vaginal sex, 306–307

Making out. *See* Low-risk sexual activities
Male, 67
Male anatomy, 71–72
Male-ness. *See* Biological sex
Mammogram, 83
Man-ness. *See* Gender identity
Margaret, 12
    on being raped, 227
    on birth control, 109
    on communication, 147
    on masturbation, 290
    on pregnancy, 109
    on problems in a relationship, 199
    on same-sex attraction, 63
Marital rape, 224, 235
Marriage
    rights concerning, 229
    virginity at, 245
Masculine. *See* Gender expression
Masochism, 319–320, 323
Masturbation, 275–290
    Blake's diary entry on, 278–279
    different perspectives on, 275–276
    Erin's diary entry on, 288
    instead of engaging in other activities/
    relationships, 283
    Jordan's diary entry on, 281

Lina G.'s diary entry on, 289
in managing orgasms, 267
Margaret's diary entry on, 290
myths and truths about, 276–277, 280
as normal activity, 314–315
positive aspects of, 275
reasons for not wanting, 283
and religion, 287
safety concerns with, 282–283
types of activities involved in, 280, 282
when in relationships, 287
May, Emmeline, 219–223
Menstrual cup, 76
Menstrual cycle, 73–76
Messaging, flirting when, 293
Microaggressions, 58–59
Monogamy, 216, 217
Mons veneris, 71, 78–80, 349
Morally wrong sexual activities, 313
Morning-after pill, 121, 122
Mosaic Turner syndrome, 69
Motivations, for hooking up, 178–179
Multiple orgasms, 269

Nakedness, comfort with, 248
National Domestic Violence Hotline, 165, 168
Natural family planning, 123
Negative sexual activities, 227–240
legal implications of, 228
rape, 235–239
and rights of individuals, 228–229
sexual assault, 232–240
sexual harassment, 230–231
social implications of, 228
Nervous system, 72
New partners
firsts with, 250–253
oral sex with, 302, 304
talking about fantasies with, 318
New Relationship Energy (NRE), 189–190
No means no rule, 224, 232
Nonverbal communication, 17–18
"Normal" sexual activities, 314–315
NRE (New Relationship Energy), 189–190

"The one," finding, 201
Online life, 21–25
being you online, 21–22
non-consensual posting of pictures, 24
problems faced in, 22–24
Oral sex, 302–305
Lina G.'s diary entry on, 303
as rape, 235–236

Orgasms, 77, 257–273
Anjali's diary entry on, 272–273
biology of, 260–262
Blake's diary entry on, 270
cultural assumptions about, 265–267
ejaculations and, 268–269
inability to experience, 267
Jordan's diary entry on, 259
knowing if partner has had, 269, 271
language around, 257
Lina G.'s diary entry on, 263
managing, 267
multiple, 269
non-ejaculating, 269
physical sensations with, 258, 260
to prepare for first penetrative sex, 248
psychology of, 262–264
during rape, 238
and touching, 298–299
vaginal vs. clitoral, 262, 264
value assigned to, 265
Origin stories, 36, 40
Outer labia, 70, 71, 349
Ovary(-ies), 70, 349
Ovulation, 74

Pads, 75, 76
Pain
in BDSM, 319
of penetration, 244–246
vaginal, 267
Pansexual, 49
Panty liners, 75
Pap test, 83
Parasitic STIs, 95–96
Parenting, 116–118
Parents, 9, 40–41
coming out to, 35, 55
gender role assumptions by, 41–42
of partners, meeting, 248
Partner(s)
communicating about orgasms with, 271
first sexual experiences with, 250–256
gender assumptions of, 42
for hooking up, 177–178
meeting parents of, 248
new. See New partners
orgasms of, 269, 271
sharing sexual fantasies with, 317–318
who are not "out" yet, 166, 167
Pelvic exam, 83–84
Penetration/penetrative sex
anal sex, 305

in definition of rape, 235
dildos for, 323
as emotionally/physically taxing, 307
first, pain and, 244–246
making decisions about, 247–248
and orgasm, 261–262
sexual activities not involving, 307
talking with friends about, 251
vaginal sex, 306
Penis, 70–72, 349
cleanliness of, 80
ejaculations from, 268, 269
and masturbation, 282
oral sex on, 304
and orgasms, 261, 262
and painful penetration, 246
refractory period for, 269
self-exam of, 82
People you spend time with, 19, 21
Perineum, 71, 349–350
Period(s), 73–74. See also Menstrual cycle
paraphernalia for use during, 75–76
PMS during, 75
Period underwear, 76
Physical appearance. See Appearance
Physical exams
annual, 83–84
self-exams, 81–83
Physical risks, of hooking up, 176
Pictures, sexually suggestive, 24
The pill, 121, 122
Placenta, 111
Plan B, 121, 122
Planned Parenthood, 121, 280, 316
Platinum Rule, 203
Pleasure, 76–78
Blake's diary entry on, 278–279
cultural expectations of, 265
with orgasm, 258
and self-perception, 264–266
from touching, 298–299
during vaginal penetration, 306
Plus (in LGBTQ+), 48
PMDD (premenstrual dysphoric disorder),
75
PMS (premenstrual syndrome), 75
Poly, 50
Pornography, 320–323
erotica vs., 322–323
ethical consumption of, 321
positive perspectives on, 321–322
problems with, 320–321

revenge porn, 24
Posture, 17–18
Pre-exposure prophylaxis (PrEP), 93
Pregnancy, 107–126
biology of, 108, 110–111
continuing pregnancy and finding
adoptive parents, 118
continuing pregnancy and parenting,
116–118
fear of, 108
good things and hard things with,
107–108
Lina G.'s diary entry on, 114
making decisions about, 111–120
Margaret's diary entry on, 109
and menstrual cycle, 74
options with, 111–112
preventing, 120–123
from rape, 238
terminating, 112–116
Premenstrual dysphoric disorder (PMDD),
75
Premenstrual syndrome (PMS), 75
PrEP (pre-exposure prophylaxis), 93
Presenting yourself. See also Brand
authenticity in, 25–26
in face-to-face interactions, 15–16
online, 21–22
Pressure
to be in a relationship, 197
for hookups, 179
Prevention
of pregnancy, 120–123
of sexually transmitted infections,
102–103
Privacy laws, for online information, 24
Private relationships, 196
Problems
ending relationships because of, 207
in online life, 22–24
in relationships, 198–200, 202
Procrastination, 333
Prom, asking someone to, 187
Property, females as, 244
Prostate, 71, 350
and anal sex, 305
and masturbation, 282
Psychological control, in rape, 238
Psychology
and "normal" sexual activities/identities,
314–316
of orgasms, 262–264

Puberty
change in genitalia during, 81
Erin's diary entry on, 87
marriage at, 245
menstrual cycle in, 73
Pubic bone, 70, 71
Pubic hair, 350
Pubic lice, 95
Public relationships, 194–195

Queer, 48, 61
Questioning, 48
Questions, practicing answers to, 329–330

Rape, 235–239
attempted. See Sexual assault
definitions of, 235–236
legal implications of, 228
Margaret's diary entry on, 227
marital, 224, 235
moving forward from, 237
and rape culture, 237–239
reporting, 236–237
Rape culture, 237–239
Real life
authenticity in, 25–26
experiencing fantasies in, 317
porn sex vs., 320
sexuality in, 329–333
Rectum, 70, 71, 80
Redress, right to, 229
Refractory period, 269
Regrets, 177
Rejection, when asking someone out, 185
Relationships. See also specific types of
relationships, e.g.:Hooking up
balancing your authenticity with others'
expectations in, 26
being in. See Being in a relationship
ending. See Ending relationships
in Fifty Shades of Grey, 323
finding balance in, 201–203
gender and, 36
healthy. See Healthy relationships
long-term, 203
masturbating instead of engaging in,
283
masturbation when in, 287
New Relationship Energy, 189–190
private aspects of, 196
public aspects of, 194–195
in real life, 329–333
rights concerning, 229
societal and cultural norms for, 37–40

types of, 143–144
unhealthy, 161–168
Religion
and abortion, 113
and homophobic subcultures, 58
and masturbation, 287
Religious adoption agencies, 118
Remedies, right to, 229
Reporting sexual assault and rape, 236–237
Reproductive organs, 69
Resolution, to relationships that drift apart,
214–215
Respect
definition of, 158
in relationships, 158–161
when ending relationships, 205
Revenge porn, 24
Rhythm method, 123
Rights of individuals
concerning painful activities, 245–246
concerning sexual activities, 228–229.
See also Consent
concerning sexual harassment, 231
Right thing, doing the, 332
Ring contraceptive, 121
Risks. See also Low-risk sexual activities
with condoms, 247
in hooking up, 171–172, 175–177
and masturbation, 282–283
of random sex with new people, 248,
250
in reporting rape or sexual assault, 236
with sexual activities, 247
talking with new partner about, 251
when consent is unclear, 226
Role-plays, 330
Romance
and balance in relationships, 201, 203
and logistics, 203
Romantic attraction, 50–52. See also
Attraction; Relationships
Rookie, 320
Roosevelt, Eleanor, 332

Sadism, 319–320, 323
Safety
with BDSM, 320
definition of, 158
and masturbation, 282–283
in relationships, 158–161
and reporting rape or sexual assault,
236

of sexual fantasies, 317
topics related to, 247
in using sex toys, 323–324
Same-gender relationships, gender role
  assumptions in, 42–43
Scabies, 95
Scarleteen, 280, 307, 320
School environments
  sexual harassment in, 230
  Slap Ass Fridays, 232, 234
The Science of Kissing (Sheril
  Kirshenbaum), 298
Scrotum, 282, 350
Secondary sex characteristics, 71, 72
Self-care
  cleanliness, 78–81
  self-exams, 81–83
Self-compassion, 84, 128
Self-exams, 81–83
Self-honesty, 143–146
Self-image, ending relationships and, 209,
  211
Self-love, 84–87
  Erin's diary entry on, 87
  Lina G.'s diary entry on, 85
Self-perception
  cultural influence on, 265
  and sexual pleasure, 264–266
Self-presentation. *See* Presenting yourself
Seminal vesicles, 71, 350
Sex, 67–68
  assignment of, 67, 68
  biological, 30–34
  body parts related to, 68–73
  expressions of, 65–66
  language around, 9
  as a noun, 67. *See also* Body
  rights concerning, 228–229
  websites with accurate information
    about, 280
Sex, physical acts of. *See also* Sexual
  activities
  anal, 305–306
  Anjali's diary entry on, 254–256,
    308–310
  first time for, 254–256. *See also* Firsts
  forced. *See* Sexual assault
  instruction about, 301–302
  oral, 302–305
  penetration. *See* Penetration/
    penetrative sex
  penile-vaginal, possibility of pregnancy

with, 112
  porn sex, 320–321
  too much, 315
  vaginal, 306–307
Sex addiction, 315–316
Sexism, 301
Sex toys, 323–324
  lubricants for, 246
  during masturbation, 282
  in vaginal sex, 306
Sexual activities. *See also* specific
  activities, e.g.: Masturbation
  "abnormal," 312–314
  arousal and pleasure, 76–78
  as cheating, 216
  consent to, 219–229
  first-time. *See* Firsts
  in hooking up, 171–172, 174
  inappropriate, 312–314
  language around, 312–316
  leading to orgasm, 261–262
  low-risk. *See* Low-risk sexual activities
  negative or illegal. *See* Negative sexual
    activities
  "normal," 314–315
  not involving penetration, 307
  and penetration, 307
  resulting in fluid exchange, 96, 102–103
  and rights of individuals, 228–229
  risks in, 176–177, 251
  too much sex, 315
  wrong, 312–314
Sexual anatomy, body image in, 84–86.
  See also Body
Sexual assault, 232–240
  Blake's diary entry on, 233–234
  definition of, 232
  legal implications of, 228
  moving forward from, 237
  rape, 235–239
  and rape culture, 237–239
  reporting, 236–237
  sexual harassment vs., 232, 234
Sexual attraction, 50–52. *See also*
  Attraction
Sexual biology, 65–66. *See also* Body
Sexual decisions, 130–133
Sexual harassment, 230–231
  definition of, 230
  legal implications of, 228
  sexual assault vs., 232, 234
Sexual history, 248

Sexuality, 335–345
  body parts used to experience/express, 72
  evolution of, 335–344
  fantasies, 316–318
  Freud on, 264
  kink and fetish, 318–320
  language around, 9, 312–316
  learning and thinking about, 329–331, 338–345
  pornography, 320–323
  rarely-discussed topics of, 311
  in real life, 329–333
  rights concerning, 228–229
  sex toys, 323–324
  websites with accurate information about, 280
Sexually suggestive pictures, 24
Sexually transmitted diseases (STDs), 89–90
Sexually transmitted infections (STIs), 89–106
  Anjali's diary entry on, 104–106
  bacterial, 94–95
  Blake's diary entry on, 92
  categories of, 90
  disclosure of, 102
  Lina G. on, 97–98
  with oral sex, 302
  parasitic, 95–96
  preventing, 102–103
  stigma related to, 100–102
  testing for, 96–99, 251, 253
  viral, 90–94
Sexual orientation/identity
  coming out about, 35
  gender expression vs., 35
  and gender identity, 61–62
  heterosexual, 48
  language of, 47–50
  LGBTQ+, 48
  "normal," 314
Sexual physiology, 66. See also Body
  menstrual cycle, 73–76
  and pain with first penetration, 244
Sexual pleasure. See Pleasure
Sexual rights, 228–229. See also Negative sexual activities
Sexual violence, 228. See also Negative sexual activities
Shots, contraceptive, 121
SIV (simian immunodeficiency virus), 93

Skoliosexual, 50
Slap Ass Fridays, 232, 234
Smegma, 350
Smiling, in flirting, 292
Smith, Margaret Chase, 332
Social implications
  of being in public relationships, 194
  of negative sexual activities, 228
Social media, 20, 21. See also Online life
Social risk, of hooking up, 176–177
Societal norms, 37–40
Sodomy, forced. See Sexual assault
Spanking, 317
Spektor, Regina, 84
Spence-Chapin, 118
Spine, 70, 71
Sponge (contraceptive), 121
Starting a "thing." See Dating
STDs See Sexually transmitted diseases
Stigma
  related to STIs, 100–102
  related to unhealthy relationships, 167–168
STIs. See Sexually transmitted infections
Straight, 48
Submission, 319–320, 323
Support. See also Community
  in dealing with fantasies, 317
  in moving forward from assault/rape, 237
  for pregnant teenagers, 117
  in working through issues, 316
Surgical contraceptive methods, 122–123
Syphilis, 94–95
Systematic decision making, 136–138
Talking, 146–148
Talkline, 120
Tampons, 75–76
Teachers, relationships with, 143–144
Teenagers
  and love, 200–201
  pregnancy of, 107–108
  pregnant, supportive communities for, 117
Terminating pregnancy, 112–116
Testicles, 71, 72, 350–351
  and masturbation, 282
  and oral sex, 304
  self-exam of, 82
Testing, for sexually transmitted infections, 96–99, 251, 253
Texting, 21, 293. See also Online life

Tongue, 78
Too much sex, 315
Touch/touching
    deliberate, 299
    in flirting, 292-293
    kissing, 296-298
    during oral sex, 304
    sexual ways of, 298-299
Transgender, 34, 48
Transphobia, 56
Trichomoniasis (trich), 96
Trust, 320
    around sexual health, 216
    and cheating, 215
    definition of, 158
    in relationships, 158-161
Truths, about rape and sexual assault, 238
Tubal ligation, 122
Turner syndrome, 69
Two spirit, 50

Unhealthy relationships, 161-168
    Blake's diary entry on, 169-170
    embarrassment about, 167-168
    ending, 168, 209-210
    Erin's diary entry on, 218
    gaslighting, 164-165
    getting help with, 168
    intent in, 165-166
    Jordan's diary entry on, 162
    when partners aren't "out" yet, 166, 167
Urethra, 70-71, 351
Uterus, 70, 74, 351

Vagina, 70, 71, 78-80, 351-352
    ejaculations from, 258, 259, 261-262, 268-269
    infections of, 79-80
    in masturbation, 280, 282
    nerve endings in, 306
    in oral sex, 302, 304
    penetration of, 244-245
    pH of, 78-79
    stimulation of, 261-262

Vaginal discharge, 73-74, 82
Vaginal orgasms, 262, 264
Vaginal pain, 267
Vaginal sex, 306-307
Vas deferens, 71, 351-352
Vasectomy, 122
Vibrators, 323
Violence, 228. See also Negative sexual activities
Viral STIs, 90-94
Virginity
    cultural value of, 244, 245
    language around, 243
    Lina G.'s diary entry on, 249
Vulva, 69-72, 351-352
    cleanliness of, 78-80
    health of, 82
    in masturbation, 280
    and oral sex, 302, 304

WAS (World Association of Sexual Health), 228, 229
Well Woman exams, 83
West, Mae, 200
Who you are. See Brand; Identity
Winfrey, Oprah, 332
Withdrawal, as contraception method, 123
Woman-ness. See Gender identity
Women
    porn's degradation of, 321
    as property, 244
Work environments
    sexual assault in, 234-235
    sexual harassment in, 230, 231
World Association of Sexual Health (WAS), 228, 229
World Health Organization, 93
Wrong sexual activities, 312-314

Yeast infections, 79, 80
Yes means yes rule, 226, 232